Women Speaking,
Women Listening

FAITH MEETS FAITH

An Orbis Series in Interreligious Dialogue

Paul F. Knitter, General Editor

In our contemporary world, the many religions and spiritualities stand in need of greater intercommunication and cooperation. More than ever before, they must speak to, learn from, and work with each other, in order to maintain their own identity and vitality and so to contribute to fashioning a better world.

FAITH MEETS FAITH seeks to promote interreligious dialogue by providing an open forum for the exchanges between and among followers of different religious paths. While the series wants to encourage creative and bold responses to the new questions of pluralism confronting religious persons today, it also recognizes the present plurality of perspectives concerning the methods and content of interreligious dialogue.

This series, therefore, does not want to endorse any one school of thought. By making available to both the scholarly community and the general public works that represent a variety of religious and methodological viewpoints, FAITH MEETS FAITH hopes to foster and focus the emerging encounter among the religions of the world.

Already published:

FAITH MEETS FAITH SERIES

Women Speaking, Women Listening

Women in Interreligious Dialogue

Maura O'Neill

ORBIS BOOKS

Maryknoll, New York 10545

Library of Congress Cataloging-in-Publication Data

O'Neill, Marua.
    Women speaking, women listening : women in interreligious dialogue
Maura O'Neill.
        p.   cm. — (Faith meets faith)
    Includes bibliographical references.
    ISBN 0-88344-698-7. — ISBN 0-88344-697-9 (pbk.)
    1. Women and religion.   2. Religions — Relations.   3. Dialogue —
Religious aspects.   I. Title.   II. Series
BL458.054   1990
291.1'72'082 — dc20   90-35123
                                                                  CIP

To
my mother Mary
and
all the women who have been
a challenge and support for me

Contents

vii

Introduction

Toward a Genuine Approach to Religious Pluralism

Religious pluralism has become an issue of major importance in a world wrought with a growing population, increasing immigration, and the threat of nuclear extinction. In response, philosophers and theologians have reflected on ways in which inhabitants of this earth can both maintain their cherished truth claims and also live peacefully with those who disagree. Their work has served to challenge religious leaders, teachers, and communities to recognize and respect the validity of other ways. Their work has also precipitated the need for interreligious dialogue to increase mutual understanding and cooperation.

The thesis of this book is that while dialogue is crucial for coping with the problems of modernity, it is crippled in its effect because its base of religious pluralism is not sufficiently plural. Even as the members of the world religions begin to understand the nature of their differences and similarities, one difference has gone unnoticed for the most part: that is the difference of gender. If interreligious dialogue attempts to be plural and inclusive of what John Hick calls all the "various concrete ways of being human"[1] in the world, why have most participants in dialogue been only men? Why have not women or their theological work been taken into consideration at the dialogue table?[2] A probable response to these questions is that, for the male theologians interested in pluralism, the term *human* has been considered gender inclusive. The main contention of this book is that the female way of being human differs from the male way and that this difference is a major issue in the world's religions and cultures. As a result, when women and their ideas are not explicitly included in the dialogue, the perspective on religion is male only. What is supposed to be pluralistic is really monistic as far as gender is concerned.

At first glance, the problem would appear to have a simple solution: invite women to participate in the dialogue. On further consideration, however, reasons are discovered as to why this solution would create more problems rather than resolve the existing one. There are reasons why women have been excluded and these reasons are rooted in the androcentric philosophical underpinnings of interreligious dialogue. If this problem is not addressed, women will be facing some longstanding, yet for the most part unconscious, prejudices that will interfere with an open and honest exchange. Therefore, the first part of this book suggests that, initially, women dialogue among themselves so that their uniqueness and self-definition can be established. In so doing, the differences that exist in the various women's and men's ways of being human will be illuminated, and the issues that women need to raise will have been explored. Only then can these issues be brought to the dialogue with men and receive the hearing that is their due.

To a limited extent, women have already realized the need to come together among themselves in interreligious and intercultural dialogue. When they do, however, they encounter difficulties that are unique to them and are not always issues for their male counterparts. Hence, the second part of this book explores some of these problems for the purpose of clarifying them so that they can be anticipated and coped with in future encounters. While the risk is obvious in proposing some specific advice for an activity as open-ended as dialogue, some suggestions have been found helpful, and these are presented in Part III.

Finally, it must be stressed that these pages are not an argument for separatism. They are intended strictly as a first step in the journey towards genuine pluralism—a journey that represents mutual understanding and crosses not only religious and cultural lines but gender lines as well.

Women Speaking, Women Listening

PART I

Women and the Philosophy of Interreligious Dialogue

1

The Nature of the Human Person

OVERVIEW

Engagement in interreligious dialogue is based on certain philosophical assumptions and, therefore, is itself a philosophical endeavor. As such it should be subject to the same critique as those branches of philosophy that undergird it. Since one of those critiques derives from a feminist perspective, we can conclude that a feminist critique can also be applied directly to the topic of interreligious dialogue. The purpose here is to examine some of those critiques to determine whether or not they would warrant a separate dialogue among women alone.

Interreligious dialogue is, quite simply, persons communicating about their relationship with and experience of the ultimate reality or realities. One Christian, a member of the Lutheran World Federation, further defined such dialogue as "an encounter between religious persons, each having a particular religious experience or insight into the mysteries of God or the world."[1] Both of these definitions stress concepts that are the focal points of some very significant philosophical issues.

Philosophy provides rational and critical speculation about the most important questions. Such questions include the following:

What is the nature of persons?

What is meant by the ultimate reality?

How do we obtain knowledge of ourselves and the ultimate reality?

What is meant by religious experience?

How do we determine what is of greatest value?

Because the terms *persons, ultimate reality, knowledge* and *experience* are all crucial for defining interreligious dialogue, each of these questions needs to be addressed if the definition is to be coherent. I contend further that, in order for dialogue to take place at all, the responses to such questions must have at least a minimal amount of consensus among the participants.

In recent years, each of these philosophical questions has been critiqued by feminist philosophers who maintain that the traditional perspectives have been androcentric. Problems of gender have been found lurking in ontology, epistemology, ethics, and, to no one's surprise, in the philosophy of religion. There seems to be a consensus among scholars of both sexes that the discipline of philosophy has long excluded women, even though some industrious historians have discovered women thinkers from ages past. It also has been conceded that many of the great male philosophers of the past have had a rather condescending, if not openly misogynistic, opinion of women. Some modern students and teachers of philosophy have attempted to remedy the situation by either including women thinkers in their syllabi or by deleting those passages of the great thinkers which, these scholars say, merely reflect the social attitude of the philosophers' times and have no real bearing on the heart of their theories. Plato's cave, Descartes' method, or Sartre's bad faith could still be defined in a gender neutral way, they say. These approaches, however, are growing more and more inadequate as feminist philosophers continue their critique and discover, in the words of Linda Gardiner, "the extent to which the doing of philosophy is necessarily tied to a set of values, methods, and self-definitions which serve to exclude women (and in fact to exclude all 'outgroups' in society)."[2] The task before the philosopher who is seeking to move beyond androcentrism seems overwhelming when one realizes that the entire foundation upon which our social, political, scientific, and metaphysical systems are based is patriarchal and needs to be shaken up.

It seems that the solution lies not only in the addition of women and women's ideas into the subject matter, but also in the revision of the academic disciplines themselves.[3] This idea of a radical revision of philosophy keeps appearing in many women's works and can be summed up economically in the words of Sheila Ruth:

> Male voices, perspectives, interests, ideas, and modes dominate all thinking. For all intents and purposes, "official" intellection and male intellection have become coextensive. In the realm of thought the male is universalized. As a result the categories of relevance have been appropriated by the male frame of reference: . . . That which is of importance is [what the male perceives as important]; . . . Not only have women had no part in defining the content of philosophical speculation, but they have had even less influence over the categories of concern and the modes of articulation.[4]

The following pages will look at the feminist critique of those specific questions of philosophy previously mentioned because these issues have direct bearing on the process of interreligious dialogue. The implication here, and the conclusion later, is that all of this careful examination by feminist philosophers adds to a feminist critique of the dialogue itself. The implications of this critique will be the subject of the subsequent chapters.

The Concept of Person

The first important concept with significant philosophical implications for interreligious dialogue concerns the idea of person. Highlighting this word, Wilfred Cantwell Smith writes, "The study of religion is the study of persons ... it illumines to see [religion] humanely, actively, as a quality of personal living."[5] Unless we share a common idea of personhood, it is difficult to hold dialogue about, much less agree on, the meaning of religion as Smith describes it. Will the study of religion be the same if we are studying female persons as well as male persons within any of the world's traditions? Will our speaking and listening be the same if we are in dialogue with a female person rather than a male person?

My argument is that once we wish to become personal, we become particular, and once we become particular, we must begin to talk about gender. Although the word *person* appears to be a gender neutral term, it, in fact, is not. When Wilfred Cantwell Smith defines faith as "an inner religious experience or involvement of a particular person,"[6] it seems safe to assume that, since he does not make specific reference to male or female, he intends person to apply to both genders. I maintain, and will demonstrate that when he and other philosophers of religion refer to person, they are referring to a male model and subsume the female under this definition.

Both Raimundo Panikkar and John Hick are noted for their discussions of pluralism which are focused not so much on doctrinal definitions as on the human experience of one divine reality. Panikkar writes that "Religions meet in the heart rather than in the mind ... [in] the concrete reality of our lives ... [in] the heart of the *person.*"[7] Again, since he makes no specific reference to male or female hearts, it is safe to say that Pannikar intends this statement for both. John Hick uses a similar all-inclusive concept of person in his theory of the test for the validity of religious experience. He believes that a religion can be considered to be a valid expression of the divine reality if it leads a person to transform her or his "existence from self-centeredness to Reality-centeredness."[8] Again, Hick intends this test to apply to both men and women, but can it? I believe that these and other theorists need to be critiqued in light of current philosophical work. Only then will it be understood that their use of the concept *person* is, in actuality, referring solely to the male gender. If this be so, then current work on pluralism and dialogue cannot be considered gender neutral. We shall then have to say the same about the dialogue process that feminists have said about philosophy in general: "Male voices, perspectives, ... ideas and modes dominate all thinking."[9]

FEMINIST THEORIES

Current feminist thinkers are reexamining the history of Western thought to discover the underlying influences and suppositions that modern philosophers work with. Feminist theorists are also posing new questions which might open the way to a more inclusive interpretation of the word *person*.

These women have concentrated on the idea of person because it is so central to all philosophical endeavor and because the concept has been so often misunderstood. Those using the term claim it to be inclusive. However, in reality, such references generally mean just the male and the term still marks the female as inferior. Sandra Harding in her work on the philosophy of science writes:

> Many philosophers, drawing on the received wisdom of their day, explicitly explained why women are by nature less able or less willing to satisfy criteria for full human personhood. . . . Recent studies show that such attempts to "clean up" the history of philosophy by detaching claims about sex/gender differences from the rest of a philosopher's arguments are both wrongheaded and also doomed to failure. They fail because no social characteristic is more basic to individual self-identity than a sense of gender . . . Of all social characteristics, gender is the earliest to be solidified in the individual, the hardest to change, and the most inextricably connected with how we conceptualize and relate to ourselves, to others, and to nature.[10]

Harding is saying that genders were always viewed differently and, therefore, were factored into philosophical theory with the result that women have been relegated to an inferior status. Gender has played a role in determining social relations and individual identity; therefore, its importance in defining the human person must be acknowledged. Once it is, however, many problems and conflicts result. For example, what determines gender and what are the particular gender differences? Are these differences biological, hence innate or natural? Or are they culturally determined, in which case they would be changeable? If changeable, then would not social relations and individual identity also be subject to change, and would not the position of women have to be reconsidered and reevaluated?

One of the existing debates on the subject is between the Essentialists and the Relativists. The Essentialists are convinced that sex differences in the sense of gender refer to concrete, biological distinctions between men and women.[11] Many feminist researchers contend that this theory about the sexes is part of a dominant ideology that impedes any understanding of a society's construction of the sexes.[12] The Essentialist position leads to a belief in biological determinism that, as its name implies, means that biological differences determine behavior, social structure, and social policy. Therefore, roles are relatively unchangeable.[13] Thus a prevalent idea maintains that because the woman bears the children and lactates for the infant's nourishment, her role is mother, and because of this role she is designated the primary nurturer, which defines her place as in the home and by implication in the private sphere. Therefore, women in the work force, politics, or ministries are considered to be doing that which is against their nature. In this perspective, it is biology that basically determines sex differences and, therefore, personal identity and behavior in all other aspects of life. In other words, personhood is rooted in biology.

The Relativists, on the other hand, take the opposite position and believe that sexuality is a social construction. Culture determines sexual characteristics and gender roles. Therefore, these aspects of personhood are not immutable but can be changed either by changing environmental conditions or by human strategies.

More recent feminist philosophers have challenged both of these positions. The argument they put forth is that there exists a dialectical and historical relationship between biology and culture. Although biological traits have influenced the social order, it is also true that general physical structure as well as hormonal differences are partly the product of human social evolution. They, too, need to be understood in a cultural context.

One such philosopher, Jean Grimshaw, explains this theory when she writes:

> Sexual difference itself is not something which is simply given; it is something which can change historically and is conditioned by culture. But neither is sexual difference or reproductive difference simply reducible to culture . . . Though it seems to me to be likely that there will always be some difference, it does not follow from this that any particular difference is determined.[14]

Contrary to some popular opinions, not all feminists wish to do away with the distinction between the sexes. Rather, it is the nature of such distinctions and the value placed on them that are the targets of feminist criticism. Those stereotypical characteristics that lie inherent when the term *person* is used must be reconsidered and altered.

If biology and culture are and have been in a dialectical relationship, it follows that no particular human activity is merely natural.

Another proponent of this dialectical theory is Alison Jaggar, who explains that human biology is not a given that has remained constant throughout the changes in human social life. Instead, it is an effect as well as a cause of our system of social organization. Examples of biology being changed by environment include the evolution of human reproductive biology.

> In the course of human evolution, the development of bipedalism narrowed the pelvis and reduced the size of the bony birth canal in women. Simultaneously, however, tool use selected larger brain size and consequently larger bony skulls in infants. This "obstetrical dilemma" of large-headed infants and small birth canals was solved

by the infants' being born at an earlier stage of development. But this solution was possible only because human social organization was developed sufficiently to support a long period of infant dependence.[15]

Jaggar also proposes that the relatively smaller size of females in some ethnic groups is due to the fact of lower social status. She then quotes Andrea Dworkin, who believes that even the biological sex differences themselves may be in part a social product. Her argument is that since individuals who were "inter-sex" or lacking clearly defined sex distinctions were less likely to be preferred as marriage partners, they gradually disappeared in the process of natural selection.[16] Jaggar's conclusion is that "we cannot identify a clear, nonsocial sense of 'biology' nor a clear, non-biological sense of 'society.' "[17]

Accepting this theory as true has ramifications for the position of women in society because we would have to concede that no social role hitherto dictated by gender is any more "natural" or biologically predetermined than any other. In other words, the bearing of children is not an indicator that woman's predetermined task is homemaker and childraiser. Likewise, because the male is biologically larger and stronger does not mean that he is predetermined to be the protector and provider who works outside the home. Thus the traditional line of demarcation between the public and private spheres can no longer be so clearly drawn or so clearly identified with one sex or the other.

An alternative way of describing this dichotomized relationship between biology and society is to use the terms nature vs. culture. Nature here refers to those biological aspects of humans that are shared with the animal world; by contrast, culture refers not only to the conditions in which the persons live but also to the distinctively human manipulation of those conditions. These terms imply a further dimension to the dichotomy that compounds the problem from the woman's perspective—the dimension of power. Culture implies the social conditions which impose constraints on human nature: a thought which echoes Freud's theory of war between culture and instinct. However, whether nature is something to be feared as in the philosophy of Hobbes or is something to be freed as in Rousseau, culture acts as its constraint. If, as was seen in previous pages, nature and woman are linked, then the culture that controls is male. This dichotomy is further explained by Brown and Jordanova, who write

The distinction between nature and culture is basic to recent Western thought . . . a distinction between unmediated, intractable nature, and a realm of human mastery where conscious social and individual action is accorded an important measure of power . . . Western traditions lay particular emphasis on controlling nature by means of culture, especially through science, medicine and technology.[18]

Today, a cult of experts can be found to give advice on the latest and most effective way to conduct even the most personal of human activities. There is a scientific method to finding your mate, making love, giving birth, raising children, and solving arguments. This specialized technological society has increased the degree of control that culture holds over nature.

In sum, woman has been identified with nature and those physical characteristics that are shared with the animal world. She is therefore emotional, subject to hormonal variation, and less capable of self-control. As such, she is somewhat lower on the scale of full rational humanity and therefore needs to be controlled by culture.

Reason vs. Nature

This last statement leads to the consideration of another major dichotomy in the exploration of the meaning of the human person: the dichotomy between reason and nature, or, in other words, between mind and body. Throughout the history of Western philosophy, the rational capacity has been understood as the element that distinguishes the human being from other life forms. That the male and female both equally possess this uniquely human characteristic appears to have escaped many philosophers of ages past. Evidence for this judgment is contained in a text entitled *The Man of Reason: 'Male' and 'Female' in Western Philosophy* by Genevieve Lloyd. Her detailed study of major philosophers reveals that deeply rooted in their work is the concept that women were indeed viewed as less rational, and therefore as less human, than men. For example, according to Descartes, reason was associated with the realm of pure thought, which provided the foundations of science. In a world where male and female distinctions were very sharp, this separation of pure thought from practical affairs of everyday life "opened the way to the idea of a distinctive male and female consciousness."[19] Such a distinctiveness also brings with it a value judgment as to which consciousness could better seek truth and therefore which consciousness represents the highest form of human capabilities.

Lloyd also does an interesting analysis of Hume, Kant, and Hegel, in which she exposes a very gender specific, male meaning to their concepts of reason. Kant's moral philosophy, for example, splits "human life, on the one hand, into truly moral universal concerns, and on the other, into the particularities of the merely personal."[20] Since only the theoretical use of reason gives rise to moral principles and since this faculty opposes the merely personal as male opposes female, Kant has implicitly contributed to the idea of the lesser moral development of women.

In his *Foundations of the Metaphysics of Morals*, Kant explains that the source of moral law or "the ground of obligation . . . is placed a priori solely in the concepts of pure reason."[21] The qualities of sympathy for others and joy in making others happy have, according to Kant, no true moral worth. Only when an action is done out of duty without any accompanying natural inclination or sensibility does it have "genuine moral worth."[22] Here, Kant expresses his rationalistic moral philosophy in which the impartial knowledge of one's duty is the indicator of right action and the qualities of care, compassion, or other emotions detract from this duty.

If we consider the social definitions of male and female that prevailed in Kant's day and even in our own, a connection can be made between Kant's ideas and male and female virtues. Such a connection is made by Lawrence Blum in a paper published in the *Canadian Journal of Philosophy* of June 1982. Because Kant emphasizes the "male" virtues, such as objectivity and impersonalism, and deemphasizes or denigrates virtues that can be called "female," i.e., compassion, human care, concern and sympathy, there is an "acceptance in Kant of a male-centered view of social reality. ... Thus the qualities seen as comprising the morally good person are intimately related to those which society allots to men."[23]

Thus, according to Blum, Kant's philosophy does imply women's inferior moral status: women are "incapable of deep thought and of sustained mental activity against obstacles, qualities connected with reason and self-discipline such as are (in Kant's view) essential to morality."[24] That Kant viewed women this way is corroborated by Arnulf Zweig, who published Kant's philosophical correspondence. Commenting on letters about the problems of a young woman who sought his counsel, Zweig writes that Kant warns of "what happens to ladies when they think too much and fail to control their fantasies."[25]

Genevieve Lloyd has also reflected critically on other major figures in Western philosophy. Her conclusion is that "Many of [the past philosophers] did indeed believe that women are less rational than men; and they have formulated their ideals of rationality with male paradigms in mind."[26] Her work provides a backdrop for the current feminist critique of the traditional dualism envisioned between reason and nature. (Nature in this context means that which is nonhuman and is connected to the earth and the other lower life forms.) Writers such as Betty Friedan in *The Feminine Mystique* (1965) and Kate Millett in *Sexual Politics* (1977) explore the idea that woman's identity has been relegated to the sphere of "nature" and her activity to domesticity and childrearing, and that this identification has caused her to be considered somehow less than human.

Different schools of feminism have chosen to react differently to this historic dualism. Some have maintained the inferior role of nature or the physical aspects of life and have chosen to improve the place of woman by identifying her with reason; hence, women are to become more like men, more objective, more cerebral, and more in control of their emotions. Some feminists, by contrast, have chosen to maintain woman's identification with the physical realm, but have raised the importance and value of this realm, thus raising the value of women as well. A woman is still characterized by her emotion and sensitivity, but contrary to the thought of Kant, emotion and sensitivity are essential virtues on a par with impartial reason.

Both of these positions, however, are currently under criticism by a new school of women philosophers who are attacking not just women's role but the very foundations upon which the original dichotomy between reason and nature was made in the first place. In her work *Philosophy and Feminist Thinking*, Jean Grimshaw explains that no human activity can be considered more "natural" than any other. The activities of sexual intercourse, giving birth, and rearing children are human in the sense that they take place within a psycho-social context which, for better or worse, has been influenced by mental processes. Whom one has sex with, whether one has a natural birth or a Caesarean section, and how one weans the baby are determined by those capacities traditionally considered rational. By the same token, activities such as figuring math problems, planning the future, and even doing philosophy are still affected by one's physicality. In Grimshaw's words, "Human life is always embodied."[27]

In summary, the consideration of gender in defining human personhood leads to a reconsideration of the traditional dichotomies of biology vs. culture and nature vs. reason. These dualisms are, as the feminist philosopher Nancy Tuana points out, "more than mere distinctions made for pragmatic convenience, but are seen by their defenders to be metaphysically or ontologically basic. ... [and] An ontological dichotomy is an unbridgeable split."[28] Moreover, these dualisms are also ontologically significant because the very nature and definition of each term is determined by its opposition to its related term.[29] Because philosophers and other academicians have placed such emphasis on one side of these dualisms, the other side—that which has been associated with women—has often been neglected or devalued but yet has been used to define the nature of masculine, its opposite. If women's position is to change, not only do the words have to change but also the ontological underpinnings of these dichotomies. Philosophers such as Nancy Tuana and Caroline Whitbeck are accordingly calling for an ontology based on the interactions going on in us and around us. They contend that these dynamic interactions (not the opposition of dichotomized factors) are what determine the meaning of *person*. Tuana proposes

> a metaphysic compatible with current understanding of the relation of gene, environment, and organism. [She suggests] that only a process metaphysic, embodying a rich notion of interaction, is adequate to serve as a basis for the view that all observable features of an individual result from the interaction of the genetic makeup of the individual and the environment in which it develops. ... The interactions going on in us and around us then [are] what there *is*.[30]

While the scientist, to some extent, has explored the possibility of nature not being completely distinct from nurture in the development of the person, the philosopher needs to take this step also in the very definition of *person*.

In other words, all of the dualisms that are encountered in the description of person, including those of nature vs. culture and reason vs. nature, do not have a basis in the ontological reality of gender. They are, rather, words arbitrarily defined and used to distinguish different features of the common nature shared by everyone. Perhaps this type of world view will eventually shift the concept of person sufficiently so that woman and man will no longer be associated with a dichotomized reality.

What does all this metaphysical speculation have to do with the process of interreligious dialogue? The answer can be formulated into the following argument. Premise 1: Attitudes about the nature of persons effect social relationships and structures. Premise 2: Interreligious dialogue is made up of social relationships and structures. Conclusion: Therefore, attitudes about the nature of persons affect interreligious dialogue. The traditional dualisms have governed male and female roles, which in turn have determined how society is structured both politically and economically. In other words, woman's exclusion from the public sphere and her placement in the domestic role have been based on certain philosophical assumptions that have been maintained in interreligious dialogue.

This dialogue has, for the most part, been conducted by those who are not only philosophers and practitioners but also respected public representatives of their traditions. That these persons are male is a result of the philosophical legacy left to them; they, in turn, will bear the legacy to the future. I maintain that the absence of women in the past and the overlooking of them in the present are due to the deep-seated views of woman's nature discovered in the philosophical enterprise. The ontology of person is relevant and the ontology of person must be rethought.

2

Epistemology

EXPERIENCE AND GENDER

One cannot study the nature of reality without also examining how we come to know this reality. Indeed, one must determine whether or not it is even possible to know this reality. The history of epistemology reflects a gradual moving from the certainty of objective knowledge to a skepticism that doubts knowledge of any reality. This skepticism has decreased our ability to be dogmatic in any area of belief. The notion of truth has come to be deabsolutized by the changing epistemologies of the past two centuries. The observer is actually an interpreter whose perception of truth is affected by time, geography, culture, and language. Thus all truth is interpreted truth.

This deabsolutizing has had a positive effect on the process of interreligious dialogue, which had been so impaired by the absolute-truth claims of the participants. However, these same participants in the dialogue are not willing to adhere to a completely relativistic notion of truth. Hence, a dilemma arises. How does one maintain the validity of one's religious commitment while still recognizing its limited certainty?

Leonard Swidler, in examining the epistemology of dialogue, suggests an escape from total relativity in the theory that we share a common humanity. Because this common humanity is the basis for our perceptions of reality and values, we do have a springboard for dialogue that grounds us in our search for truth. Swidler generally assumes that all human beings experience certain things in common such as pain, pleasure, hunger, satiation, affection, dislike, and so forth. Such common experiences form a basis for a universal epistemology.[1]

Although feminist philosophers also attempt to avoid total relativism, they still strongly criticize the type of solution made by Swidler. While he and the major epistemologists whom he cites admit to the relativity of knowledge along historical, cultural, and linguistic lines, they nonetheless do not consider gender an issue.

Some modern feminists support the hypothesis that the way we know things and the objective truth of that which we know are very much gender related. Sandra Harding, for example, critiques the modern epistemologies from a feminist perspective and foresees the need to develop "gender-free theories."[2] She argues that

the substance of feminist claims and practices can be used to undercut the legitimacy of the modernist epistemologies, which explicitly ignore gender while implicitly exploiting distinctively masculine meanings of knowledge-seeking. Gender-sensitive revisions of modernist epistemologies have provided the main justificatory resources for feminism.[3]

What is meant by masculine epistemology? Feminist writings vary in their explanations, but three specific characteristics of male ways of knowing can be summarily identified: (1) they are based on male experiences not necessarily shared by women, (2) they are heavily dependent on the reason vs. intuition dichotomy and (3) they hold to the possibility that, through the use of reason, at least some parts of the world can be known objectively; that is, as they really are.

Experience is not only mediated by time and location but also by the gender of the subject. Thus, the first of the feminist critiques of the epistemological endeavor consists of the recognition that men's experience is different from women's experience, and if knowledge is based on experience, is not the knowledge different as well? The claims to social and natural knowledge are formed on only partial human experience which itself is only partially understood. If male experience is taken to be human experience, then the theories, concepts, and methodologies which result from this knowledge would distort human social life and human thought.[4]

When John Locke developed his empiricism explaining that all knowledge comes through experience, certainly he assumed a universal experience that applies to both men and women. Today, with advances in the field of psychology and particularly the psychology of women, Locke's claim appears simplistic. Even so, while psychologists continue to research the gender differences in experiences, epistemologists are still reluctant to acknowledge the application of these differences to their discipline. Could it be that the revolution which could result would be too catastrophic?

In her book *For the Record*, Dale Spender clearly sees the connection between men's experience and the accepted modern epistemology. Her words are striking and her point, forceful.

Men have developed the mode of thinking in our society on the basis of their experience, so it is precisely the experience of women—IF IT STANDS IN CONTRADICTION TO THE MALE VIEW OF THE WORLD—which is omitted or ignored. If we want to have women's experience incorporated then we have to change the way society thinks. This means that feminists have a vested interest in understanding the processes of thinking and reasoning, and, in order to develop a feminist theory, have to begin by exploring and explaining human consciousness and the reasons why the vast, varied and valid realms of human experience that pertain to women have been left out.[5]

What we know, says Spender, is what is known by men. Men experience and then relate that experience as though it is universally true for both sexes. They provide explanations and proofs, expecting that these theses have produced an adequate understanding of the world.

Not only are the experiences that underlie our knowledge different for men and for women, but the reasoning process by which these experiences become integrated into our knowledge is also differentiated by gender. The history of Western philosophy understands this reasoning process as a distinctively human characteristic. Whether the content of our reasoning comes from experience, as thought by the empiricists, or from innate ideas, as thought by the rationalists, we nevertheless are gifted with the ability to reason.

As Genevieve Lloyd notes, men have always been considered to have a greater degree of reasoning power than women. Women's main source of knowledge became known as intuition. Intuition, of course, is not that which Descartes valued so highly and which he equated with those sublime innate ideas that give us certain knowledge of such essential concepts as causality and morality. Rather, it is a nonrational function whose significance was demeaned as our modern society put greater and greater emphasis on the scientific mode of knowing; that is, on the empirical search for the objective truth about nature and the universe. Carol McMillan, another feminist philosopher exploring epistemology, writes that "the deprecatory attitude towards the so-called intuitive faculty of women is symptomatic of a more general prejudice against those forms of knowledge that are nonscientific in character."[6]

The theory that envisions a dichotomy between reason and intuition has been under scrutiny by feminists because, like most dichotomies, its parts have acquired gender identities and it thus serves to divide and separate the sexes. In McMillan's careful critique of this dualistic epistemology, she illustrates that those activities traditionally attributed to "man's" animal nature—such as sex and procreation—really require reasoning ability if they are to be performed by the human person. By the same token, the most intellectual of activities also can be viewed as incorporated in the more feeling or intuitive side of human nature:

> Reason . . . is not a separate faculty operating in isolation from, and in contradistinction to, man's "animal nature"—his feelings and his "instinct" for food, sex and procreation—but shows itself in the character and the role that such needs may play in his life as a whole . . .

often the use of such terms as "reason," "intellectual faculty" or "consciousness" to denote man's distinctiveness leads to talk not about real human beings but about disembodied, pure intelligence, so that reason becomes hypostatized as something existing by itself, outside any human activity or institution.[7]

Such dualistic thinking causes women to be excluded or at best tolerated in an academic setting comprised mostly of men. The suggestion that McMillan puts forth here is that woman's exclusion isn't due to any aversion towards women per se but rather to a narrow concept of reason. Men are convinced that an issue cannot have been thought through sufficiently unless one can produce a sophisticated system of laws and theories as explanation. McMillan, on the other hand, demonstrates that the use of intuition in the attainment of knowledge does not suggest that such knowledge excludes thought and sustained effort.[8] Intuition is valuable and important, as valuable and important as abstract reasoning. Moreover, these two ways of knowing, according to feminist epistemologists, need not be looked upon as two separate faculties employed in the attainment of knowledge but rather as two complementary aspects of how we come to know.

Furthermore, in the past, not only was this purely intellectual reasoning considered the only acceptable way to pursue truth, but it was also believed to yield dispassionate objectivity when it entailed observation of nature and that which lay outside itself. However, in recent times the idea of objective knowledge has been critiqued and challenged by thinkers who hold that knowledge is socially constructed. Even though philosophers such as Thomas Kuhn do suggest that science be viewed as a social enterprise, they disregard gender as part of the social factors that influence the findings of the scientist. Sandra Harding points out that these men "have systematically avoided examining the relationship between gender and science in either its historical or sociological dimensions."[9] What Harding is implying here and has stated elsewhere is that there can be a feminist epistemology: a way of knowing that is distinct from what has been and that, it is hoped, will lead the way to what can be, and what can be not just for women but for all persons.

One theory of how the acquisition of knowledge can be gender related is put forth by Evelyn Fox Keller in an essay entitled "Gender and Science."[10] Keller explains the psychological process by which nature is objectified and the result of such a process, which is that the subject interacts with nature "through reason rather than feeling, and 'observation' rather than 'immediate' sensory experience."[11] This objectification of nature—the setting apart of the known and the knower—has been characterized in Western philosophy as masculine. This characterization connotes autonomy, separation, and distance, or "a radical rejection of any commingling of subject and object."[12] This mode of knowing has been accepted as a "model of cognitive maturity"[13] by classical science which values the objectivity of the subject. However, contemporary developments have demonstrated the classic model to be inadequate. There are calls for a more sophisticated epistemology which will explain and support a dynamic conception of reality.[14]

My conclusion here is that science has provided the model for much of the work that has been done in theology and the philosophy of religion. Objectification has been an important goal for those looking for a way to understand the divine reality and the person's relationship to that reality. Even the works of the phenomenologists suggest that there is an objective way to experience or perceive. In his preface to *Religion in Essence and Manifestation*, van der Leeuw writes that his work is a "cooperative effort towards the accurate apprehension of the phenomena."[15] The phenomena, when accurately perceived, become the bases for doctrines that are meant to apply to all God's people, regardless of sex, race, or even religion.

When theologians grapple with the challenging task of understanding and explaining religious pluralism, they often begin by looking for some objective reality to which all religions could relate. They seek some doctrine or unifying experience to provide a common ground: some norm which can be used to test the validity of religions and religious experience. This search already presupposes an epistemology of distance between object and subject. Proponents of such theories believe that somehow we can come to a non-passionate way of viewing other religions as well as our own, if we can but review and rename our experience and see its similarity to the experiences of others in the world. If we call God the Ultimate Reality then we can share something in common with other religions that also believe in an ultimate reality.

But this attitude toward the objectification of knowledge, especially in the fields of theology and philosophy of religion, also has political implications. The idea of knowledge as power, a dominant theme of Michel Foucault and others, has been particularly operative in traditional theology. Feminists, as well as Latin American and Black theologians, have critiqued the attempts of Rahner, Tillich, and Barth to express something that is true for all human beings. This very attempt, claim the liberationists, has a repressive political function.[16] Sharon Welch, in her feminist theology of liberation, claims that "by focusing on the universal rather than the particular, traditional theology trivializes human suffering in history."[17] James Cone is cited as critiquing traditional theology's claim "to speak for the human as such, [while ignoring] the experience of minorities and women of all races."[18] Welch concludes that any experiences that would challenge the primacy of the universal truth claims have been ignored or made trivial by those making the claims. Liberal theology has ignored and trivialized women's experiences.

This poignant criticism can be applied to the particular discourse of interreligious dialogue. Women, women's thoughts, and women's experiences have been ignored and rendered insignificant. Considering this fact from the standpoint of feminist epistemology, I propose that women are excluded not so much because of a prejudice per se but because of the dominance of a masculine view of knowledge, reason, and objectivity.

What is all this saying? Must a feminist epistemology reject objectivity and resort to total relativism? Must we sacrifice realism for the sake of a more inclusive and less androcentric way of knowing? Presumably we would not. What, then, is the solution to knowing the truth or arriving at any foundational principle upon which understanding can be built? How do we find a peaceful place between the imposition of imperialistic truth claims and the futility of confrontation between equal yet opposing ones?

TOWARD A FEMINIST EPISTEMOLOGY

The problem of objectivism vs. relativism is being creatively explored by modern philosophers and social scientists such as Richard Bernstein and Richard Rorty whose works parallel those of feminists attempting to resolve this dichotomy. Objectivism is now being questioned because of its identification of one truth, as is Relativism because of its claim that individual frameworks can exist isolated and independent of one another. More and more modern scientists are rejecting, at least in theory, the notion of a single world. However, the notion that there are many autonomous and different worlds is also difficult to accept. The very fact that rational debate and argumentation is possible indicates that there is some overlap of observations, concepts and problems. Thomas Ommen, in his discussion of objectivism and relativism, cites the strongest attack on relativism as being the reliance on "a universal human 'bridgehead' of shared perceptions and logical standards that provide a base for translation" from one culture to another.[19] As long as people from different cultures and perspectives are able even to discuss and analyze differences, then some kind of commonality must exist, although it cannot be said to resemble anything that the objectivist might wish.

Anne Seller, in her essay "Realism versus Relativism," also claims that the realistic view of shared perceptions and standards should not be lost by feminists, because it is this epistemology that "enabled us to expose the bias and falsehood of sexist views."[20] To claim that sexism is a shared perception and that it is real, is to acknowledge that some objective reality can be known. But the question comes back to haunt us: how do we come to know the real?

In using the example of oppression to determine ways of knowing and whether knowledge is necessarily subjective or relative, Seller presents a theory to solve the dilemma, a theory that comes out of the experience of women's consciousness-raising groups. She suggests that the way to determine whether or not our perceptions are real is to discuss our experiences and decipher their meanings through defining similarities and differences between our experiences and those of other women:

> We do not have necessary and sufficient tests of the truth which we can individually apply, such as Descartes and so many since him have sought, but a process of conversation which may allow the truth to emerge, and which each of us may individually be able to judge at the end, albeit with identities and frameworks of understandings which may have only emerged through the conversation.[21]

Seller's conclusions seem to be identical to those of Ommen's study. Ommen writes, "Truth emerges . . . through conversation. . . . Meaning and truth are dependent on agreement attained in human systems of communications."[22] Ommen's analysis of epistemological theories and conversational truth-finding would lead us to believe that the above feminists' theories are not the sole property of women. Possibly, their findings can transcend the barriers of gender and serve to bridge the gap between a male and female way of knowing.

One further point that both Seller and Ommen make is extremely important to any concept of the communal knowing of truth. Seller believes that knowledge and its acquisition is ongoing: "Neither knowledge nor political solutions are final, they consist rather in continual doing . . . and that will mean continuous efforts at understanding."[23] With the input of new experience or new members of the community, what is known may change. In Ommen's words, the formulations arrived at through conversation are "hypotheses to be tested in the forum of open and unrestricted discourse."[24] The implication here is a caution for us to hold to what we know with a very relaxed grasp. While my experience of oppression may be corroborated by my sisters who have had a similar experience, and while I may hold to this truth as objective, I must also be ready to hear about and understand other forms of oppression in which I may also participate as oppressor. This I can learn only by hearing from all others.

Welch concedes the existence of two contradictory strands in feminist philosophy, both of which are necessary. On the one hand, truth claims must be limited by relativism; on the other, there is a normative claim that attempts "to identify values and structures that can transform society and end oppression."[25]

As a result of this problematic, a type of skepticism emerges that, while causing us to renounce universals, still enables the theorist to make judgments. Placing this skepticism in a historical perspective, Welch explains how she can absolutely renounce the deeds of Hitler while still doubting her own understanding of humanity. She warns that "Just as slavery and the treatment of women were for centuries not even recognized by sensitive theologians and people of faith as oppressive, it is possible that my thought and actions share in the perpetuation of as yet unrecognized forms of oppression."[26] How does one determine the objectivity of one's vision? Welch arrives at the same conclusion as Seller: what we need is conversation.

> To hold to truth as conversation rather than as reflection of essence is to live out an openness to continued change and modification, and is to relinquish the hope for and end to the conversation through the achievement of a complete understanding of liberation and justice.[27]

Thus, while no claim is made here for a full description of a feminist epistemology, we do find a hint of where to begin. One begins with conversation, a conversation entered into with an openness to hear other women's experiences as well as to express fully one's own. Then once a naming of that experience happens, one must hold a skepticism until such time as further corroboration becomes possible.

Isn't this, you say, what happens at a real interreligious dialogue? Does one have to be a feminist to arrive at a common ground by this method? It is true that in dialogue there is and has been a listening between parties. However, even though the philosophical world is grappling with alternative theories of truth, conversationalist epistemology has not yet become a part of interreligious dialogue. Ommen indicates that while some theologians have admitted that discourse has a role in the learning of theological truths, such theologians have not adequately recognized the role of interreligious dialogue as an essential part of fundamental theology.[28] Therefore, by way of challenge, I offer some questions. On what and whose experiences has the conversation been based? What form of analysis has been employed in the discussion of such experiences—an abstract intellectual procedure or one which encompasses the more direct and intuitive modes of knowing? Finally, to what extent are the proponents of the various theories of commonality willing to hold them only tentatively? To what extent is objectivity held as the goal? To what extent are subjective claims to experiential knowledge dismissed? It is the hope of feminist philosophers and theologians that eventually the posing of these questions and the tackling of the answers will cease to be a feminist endeavor and become a goal of all persons, women and men, so that a fuller human interaction can take place.

3

Value Theory

Chapters 1 and 2 leave the impression that current interreligious dialogue is abstract, analytical, and devoid of personal accounts. What can we then conclude? I would not assume that dialogue has taken this direction because women have been absent; rather, women have been absent because the traditionally feminine ways of being and knowing have been devalued.

VALUE JUDGMENTS OF MASCULINE AND FEMININE

In our discussion so far, I have observed that positive value judgments have accompanied the male pole of the dualisms of culture vs. nature and reason vs. intuition, whereas negative value judgments have attached to the female. Because of this hierarchy of values, these predominant theories can be held responsible for the subordination of women.[1] In an attempt to analyze these value judgments, feminist philosophers have produced, in the last decade, a body of theoretical work on values and value theory informed by women's consciousness and feminist concerns. The impetus for this work has been the raising of women's consciousness to the experience of oppression, an experience that has greatly shaped and informed feminist values. It has done so in two ways. First, it has caused women to criticize those values and norms by which they are judged. Second, it has caused them to reexamine the values that govern their own behavior.

Feminists have discovered that the devaluing of femaleness occurred in a structure of dominance that viewed female not as merely the other but as the inferior other. According to Genevieve Lloyd, the "equation of maleness with superiority goes back at least as far as the Pythagoreans."[2]

With regard to the dichotomies already mentioned, it has been indicated that culture has been considered good and biological nature bad; hence, culture has had to tame nature. Since women have been traditionally associated with nature, they are therefore thought to be less capable, or, to some thinkers, even incapable, of the moral development that men can achieve. Kant's attitude regarding the moral inferiority of women, discussed earlier, was also shared by philosophers and later by psychologists. Freud himself understood women to be less just than men and, according to Jean Grimshaw, he assumed the deficiency of women.[3] Grimshaw then concludes, along with other feminists, that the problem lies not with women who have not measured up to male norms but with the very norms themselves.[4]

Besides the dichotomy of culture vs. nature, there is the other split, also mentioned above, of reason vs. nature. Again, reason is more highly valued and has been traditionally associated with males. Grimshaw quotes an interesting study conducted in 1970. Here, qualities typically characteristic of men and women were evaluated, including such characteristics as "loving," "sweet," "self-assured," and "in control." Seventy-nine clinically trained psychologists, psychiatrists, and social workers, both male and female, were asked to judge characteristics they would consider indicative of mental health. One group evaluated adults (gender unspecified), another judged males, and a third group ranked females. The results showed significant correlation between the items thought to characterize *male* mental health, and those thought to characterize *adult* mental health. There was, however, very little correlation between female and adult qualities. "In other words, you cannot be *both* a mentally healthy female *and* a mentally healthy adult!"[5] Furthermore, many characteristics labeled as feminine were described in an implicitly pejorative way, such as very sneaky, unable to separate feelings from ideas, and very easily influenced.[6]

In political theory, the rational is associated with the powerful. Further, reason as a value is both the cause and the result of men possessing power. An accompanying result of a dualistic world view is that reason's so-called opposites—intuition and emotion—are devalued or even seen as bad. In her essay "Ethics Revisited," Rosi Braidotti discusses the power implications of rationality that result in domination and exclusion of the opposite. In her own words,

> I would argue ... that it is not because they are rational that men are the masters, but rather that, being the masters, they have appropriated rationality as their own prerogative. The denigration and exclusion of the feminine in philosophy, in other words, is just a pretext for the great textual continuity of masculine self-glorification: the mysterious absent entity which grants full grounds for existence to the masculine knowing subject ... The feminine is reduced to that which is "other-than" and whose difference can only be perceived in terms of pejoration and inferiority.[7]

This value judgment on the traditional dualisms also colors the opinions on public vs. private in the history of male and female work roles. The public and private generate conceptions of value and of morality that conflict; concerns seen as female have been regarded as inferior, as trivial or less important than those associated with the male sphere.[8] As a corrective, socialist feminists are attempting to unite the personal and political areas of women's lives. Feminist ethical theory seeks to integrate the personal and political aspects of personality and to institutionalize this integration.[9]

A logical consequence when the personal is devalued has been the devaluation of those forms of thinking and speaking that communicate the personal. For example, to speak out of one's experience or one's intuition is not as significant as speaking from a philosophical theory or from empirical evidence. Thus, while political theory and value theory are not themselves the subjects of interreligious dialogue, I propose that the attitudes described by the feminists working in these fields still prevail in the academic world where the philosophy of religion is explored. These attitudes have caused women to be excluded and their contributions devalued in interreligious dialogue today.

FEMINIST ETHICS

Besides critiquing the values by which women are judged by men, feminists have also critiqued the values governing their own actions. Feminist ethics is a growing field, but its inclusion in these pages is limited to an analysis of those ideas that may have direct bearing on the process of interreligious dialogue.

Several feminists have identified elements that might characterize a feminist ethic. They do not all agree, however, and various trains of thought are evident. On the one hand, Carol Gilligan's investigations reveal that women characteristically make moral decisions based on relationality as opposed to autonomy. Out of this work, she develops a feminist ethic of caring.[10] Her studies indicate that because women tend to be oriented to responsibility to and relationships with others, they find it difficult to develop a conception of their *own* rights or needs, or of responsibilities towards themselves.[11] In other words, women make moral decisions in a framework of *relationships* more than in a framework of *rights*. In her descriptions of major works in feminist ethics, Josephine Donovan views Gilligan's contribution as "the most persuasive observations about the different functioning of the female and male psyches . . . Gilligan has discovered that women's moral processing is contextually oriented."[12]

In another vein, feminist theorists such as Carol Robb and Ruth Smith have identified different elements that might characterize a feminist ethic. Such characteristics include self-determination for women, autonomy, and an inviolable sense of embodiedness.[13] These writers emphasize the idea of autonomy, which has been an important part of the claims of the feminist movement. They also stress the power of self-hood, self-determination, self-realization and becoming the subject of one's own history.[14]

To understand these two viewpoints, the origins of women's moral behavior need to be examined, especially in light of the previous conclusions on the nature of the human person. We said earlier that gender, so essential to one's identity, is neither completely biological nor completely cultural. Instead, in light of current speculation, gender is being considered the result of a dialectical relationship between these two factors. Hence, the difference in male and female ethical perspectives might also stem from the dialectical relationship between biology and culture.

An illustration of this point is found in an examination of the origins of the ethic of care and the ethic of self-determination. The ethic of care, in the eyes of many philosophers and psychologists such as Sara Ruddick and Nancy Chodorow, develops out of bearing children and the mother-child relationship at infancy. In an essay originally published in 1960 and now a well-known classic on women's ethics, Valerie Saiving discusses theories of male and female differentiation and the establishment of sexual identity. She concludes that

> the individual's sense of being male or female, which plays such an important part in the young child's struggle for self-definition, can never be finally separated from his [sic] total orientation to life; in those cases—which are the majority—in which adult men and women accept and are able to actualize their respective sexual roles, the characterological tendencies based on sex membership are reinforced and strengthened.[15]

What is being said here is that the biological processes of birth and differentiation from the mother contribute to the formation of the male's need to strive for autonomy and the female's need to strive for connectedness.

This biology is not deterministic, however, and is always interacting with the social situation. A grasp of the social situation is important if one is to understand the origin of the feminine ethic of self-determination. In oppressive societies, women have had to stress their own autonomy and self-determination in order to come out from under male domination.

What is necessary, therefore, according to Saiving, is a balance between self-giving and autonomy. But problems arise, notes Saiving, when a woman attempts to "be both a woman and an individual in her own right, a separate person some part of whose mind and feelings are inviolable, some part of whose time belongs strictly to herself, . . . [Christian] theology . . . speak[s] of such desires as sin or temptation to sin."[16] The theology to which Saiving refers is that male theology that has had to consider selfishness a sin in order to counteract the conditioning of males that can result in their being excessively independent and selfishly egocentric. This theology, when applied to women whose nature has been more relational and self-giving, results in the unhealthy loss of identity that can be crippling. Jean Baker Miller, in her study of the psychology of women, reinforces this point when she clearly states that women are so concerned about giving that their concern for self-identity is jeopardized:

Women constantly confront themselves with questions about giving ... They are upset if they feel they are not givers. They wonder what would happen if they were to stop giving, to even consider not giving? The idea is frightening and the consequences too dire to consider.[17]

Miller continues by saying that for men, "giving is clearly an added luxury that is allowed only *after* they have fulfilled the primary requirements of manhood."[18] Therefore, men consider self-giving a virtue because self-giving represents movement away from a natural tendency to selfishness. A woman, on the other hand, has been conditioned to be giving and has been reinforced in this conditioning by a religion that tells her she must strive to be more so. In this striving, woman has given herself to the point of self-abnegation, and this is what Saiving considers a sin. She sees woman's virtue, therefore, as resisting this sin, or rather, as moving toward self-identity rather than toward selflessness, thereby allowing a balance between the giving and the autonomous self. Saiving recognizes a danger in the urging of a woman to become more selfless. Such urging encourages her to be a "chameleon-like creature who responds to others but has no personal identity of her own."[19]

An analogy of the situation would be a reverse garden of Eden. Eve tempted Adam with a fruit that she held to be good, and upon eating it, Adam found it bad. Similarly, man holds out to woman the fruit of selflessness that he holds to be good, but upon swallowing it, woman finds it to be destructive.

Can these descriptions of characteristically feminine ethics be incorporated into the underlying assumptions of ethical behavior that have existed behind the dialogues of male theologians? The attitude of male theology criticized by Saiving and others appears to be very similar to the theory developed by John Hick, that transformation consists of moving from self-centeredness to reality-centeredness. Hick uses this theory as a centerpiece for his assessment of religious pluralism and as a basis for efforts to "grade religions." Its most recent elaboration appears in *An Interpretation of Religion*, published in 1989. (The original citation appeared in an article published in 1981.) Hick argues that all traditions have persons who are considered what Christians call saints, that is, persons who are "much further advanced than most of us in the transformation from self-centeredness to Reality-centeredness."[20] Gandhi is cited as a recent example of a "human being who ... realized the human moral and spiritual potential to a rare degree ... [by rising] to a new level of effective self-giving love for others."[21]

The notion of self-centeredness which, according to Hick, is in need of transformation, refers to an egoism which results from a preoccupation with self. Feminists claim, however, that this preoccupation is the resulting danger of an excessive autonomy which has been socially and naturally the characteristic of the male. If a more common feminine characteristic is relationality and self-giving, then woman's sin is more likely self-abnegation, or what Susan Dunfee calls the sin of hiding, defined as "the expending of one's vital energies not in the acceptance of one's own freedom, but in the running away from that freedom by pouring those energies into the life of another."[22] Thus we observe an essential difference between the behavior considered virtuous in traditional theology and that which the feminists consider virtuous.[23]

This distinction between a feminist and a masculine perspective on sin is also illustrated in the experience of conversion. Paula Cooey's analysis of this experience begins with a simple definition of the term: "a turning around . . . a form of spiritual transformation . . . a shift . . . from some form of bondage to being in a state of liberation."[24] Cooey notes, however, that the prevailing Christian concept of conversion has generally referred to a loss of self.

This is the concept reenforced by John Hick, who has generalized the experience in order to make it applicable to various religions. He has described the conversion experience as "the gradual transformation of human existence from self-centeredness to Reality-centeredness."[25] But, as has been described earlier, nature and culture have endowed and expected woman to be self-giving, and women, for the most part, have met this expectation. For this idea, Cooey has drawn upon Valerie Saiving's article quoted earlier, which concluded that the "underdevelopment or negation of self"[26] was woman's sin. To repent of *this* sin or to experience conversion from *this* perspective would be, therefore, very different from John Hick's experience: Hick exemplifies a perspective that, as Cooey points out "reinforces sexual stereotypes and has led to lack of sufficient attention to religious experience as a source of personal empowerment and social bonding."[27]

What, then, is the meaning of conversion when defined out of women's experience? According to Cooey,

> Conversion reflects a shift in power. It does so as a transformation from an identity based on dependence on others, such that positive worth is derivative at best, to an identity based on interdependence that allows for a positive sense of worth associated simply with being a woman and a person . . . Conversion as a turning toward "full related selfhood" is the first genuine taste for what it means to be a person equal to other persons, a full participant in a wider community of being.[28]

What Cooey has done here is to redefine both the experience of conversion and the experience of power from a feminist perspective. Granted, these differences in experiences can change as the dialectic between nature and culture evolves. Nevertheless, they are real at this moment and indicate that up to this point the definitions that male theologians and philosophers have given to these concepts cannot be taken to be universally applicable as many would wish.

If we consider the works of Gilligan, Saiving, Dunfee, and Cooey seriously, we may conclude that, for a woman, the imperative of selflessness would not lead to transformation but rather to possible self-abnegation. Hence, the description of sainthood in John Hick's schema is applicable to men but would necessarily have to be modified to include women's experience.

Aware of this feminist critique, Hick has responded to it in his recent work, *An Interpretation of Religion*. In doing so, Hick has used Valerie Saiving's article, which he quotes and then interprets as follows. He writes

> From this [Saiving's] point of view the characteristic female sin is not self-assertion but self-abnegation and failure to achieve authentic selfhood; and the function of divine grace is not so much to shatter the assertive ego as to support a weak ego towards true self-realisation . . . Because of the effects upon them of patriarchal cultures — according to this feminist analysis — many women have "weak" egos, suffer from an ingrained inferiority complex and are tempted to diffusion and triviality.[29]

From his reading of Saiving, Hick understands her as saying that self-abnegation is equivalent to failure to achieve an ego and that the main formative factor in women's lives is oppression. He then proceeds to offer his solution to the problem of women's salvation and liberation by describing how women and other oppressed persons would fit into his paradigm. He writes

> Insofar as anyone, female or male, lacks the ego-development and fulfillment necessary for a voluntary self-transcendence, the prior achievement of self-fulfilled ego may well be necessary for a true relationship to the Real. For in order to move beyond the self one has first to *be* a self.[30]

I find two basic problems with Hick's response: first, in his interpretation of the feminist analysis of women's situation, and second, in his claim that women will have to progress through two stages to achieve sainthood while men only have to pass through one.

Hick, in his interpretation of Saiving, equates the sin of self-abnegation with the failure to achieve a self. None of the feminist philosophers, at least those in the current stream of thought, say that women, either by nature or by conditioning, lack a self. What they are saying is that woman's temptation, her attraction to sin, lies in her tendency towards negation of self and her failure to tend to her own nurturing and enrichment. While this tendency has been perpetuated by a male theology and exploited by a male society, this perpetuation and exploitation happen to the self that is essentially present, to the "basic feminine character"[31] referred to by Saiving, and quoted by Hick. Therefore, when Hick interprets feminists as saying that a woman "lacks ego-development and fulfillment necessary for a voluntary self-transcendence,"[32] he is basically misunderstanding the feminist position, a position that focuses on the need for a balance in women between self-giving and withdrawing periodically in order to be nurtured and enriched.[33]

Furthermore, to suggest that women don't have a self, or that women must develop one to be able to transcend it, is, in Mary Daly's words, "grossly—indeed, ontologically—insulting."[34] Even the experience of oppression, says feminist Emily Culpepper, cannot and should not imply that women do not therefore have selves. She writes as follows:

> ... to base self-definition on our oppressed state of affairs is the essence of perpetuating a derivative, secondary and oppressive definition ... this [shock of brutal oppression] does not make the oppression the primary constitution of a woman's Self. Indeed, the oppressive conditions are a shock, a weight, a drain, precisely because they are a shock to something, a weight on something, a drain of something. That something is a sense of integrity of Self.[35]

Daly and Culpepper share the same frustration when they note that women's existence continues to be defined by her oppression and not by her positive worth and contribution to humanity. Culpepper strongly believes that "to fail to see these women's Selves is the ultimate (albeit unintended) insult."[36]

How do these ideas affect Hick's theory? If we start out with the fact that both men and women have selves, if we conclude that up to this point the dialectical relation of biology and culture has produced two different types of selves, and if we admit that the temptations to sin are different for men and women, then would we not have to conclude that the means of salvation or liberation, at this point in time, are also different for men and for women? Hick's paradigm of moving from a sinful state to a graced state, from worship of self to worship of God, may hold for men, but how would feminists interpret this paradigm? How could women be in touch with Reality, given her unique self and unique temptations? How can she have what Hick calls a "true relationship to the Real"?[37]

I believe it necessary for a female paradigm to emphasize the immanent aspect of the Real rather than its transcendence. If religions understand that the Real is near as well as far, then perhaps a woman's paradigm of the movement from sin to grace would be something like the move from the worship of others to the worship of God (reality) in self. If women, who have had a temptation to self-abnegation, were to appreciate the fact that Reality was found within them, wouldn't they be empowered in a gracefilled way? Wouldn't women then have a new sense of self? Then, perhaps, a more appropriate model of salvation would be the one suggested by June O'Connor. Rather than following the linear paradigm of Hick, she suggests a movement of balance, between self-nurturance and self-giving, a "to and fro, in and out, being with and being alone for each term of the movement (self and other) each pole of the dialectic is valuable and can provide access to, can mediate, the Real."[38] Thus, a circular model would account for polarities without causing excessive indulgence in either direction.

There is a danger in advocating these ideas, however, and it is the danger that accompanies the theorizing of all feminists. Because there is no consensus among women, there is no one view of ethical priorities or moral questions that can unproblematically be considered female. Grimshaw believes that proposing a female ethic "tends to recapitulate old polarisations, . . . which should be challenged rather than assumed."[39] This crucial warning tells us that to create another dualism of female and male ethic would be adding another brick to a building we are trying to raze. We would thus fall into the same type of thinking that we are criticizing.

At this point, also, a reminder must be inserted that the above paradigms are uniquely suited to ethics of Western traditions but would require some reworking if Buddhist and Hindu philosophies were to be considered. When members of these traditions join in dialogue, the complexity of the ethical issues increases. Both Western women and men must make their observations without overgeneralizing.

So what is the point? We must grant the fact that the above analysis of feminist ethics is not necessarily a universal one. However, doing so does not eliminate the fact that many women's experiences are significantly different from men's, so that Hick's description of transformation, whether in two stages or one, cannot be claimed as universally applying to both sexes in all religions.

In conclusion, if interreligious dialogue is going to be considered truly plural, two things must occur with regard to values: (1) women's ways of thinking and being must be given equal hearing and respect, and (2) ethical deliberations must take into consideration the different moral perspectives not only among religions but also among women and men.

4

Theology

The study of theology has been revolutionized by feminist thinking. Since it is also the area most directly relevant to interreligious dialogue, the inclusion of women's theology will radically affect the nature of such dialogue. While it is true that the concerns of many women theologians have social, political, and psychological considerations, we will focus here on a specifically religious theme that occurs frequently in feminist writing but that has been largely neglected in interreligious dialogue: gender and the nature of Ultimate Reality.

Some feminists, working within a particular tradition, have developed a feminist interpretation and defense of a traditional religious perspective on this Reality. Others, wanting to break out of the theology of their traditions, work from a broader, more philosophical perspective. They attempt to redefine Ultimate Reality out of their experience and reflection rather than out of any revelation. By examining various perspectives on the nature of the Ultimate, we can more clearly focus on the implications of gender issues for interreligious dialogue. A closer look at these perspectives—both defensive and reformist—from within different traditions needs to be taken.

The nature of the Ultimate Reality poses the greatest problem for feminists approaching Judaism and Christianity, for these religions worship a personal God who has often been thought of anthropomorphically. Even Islam, although strongly monotheistic, does not pose such a problem for feminists because, for the most part, it has ruled out the imaging of God. To understand the relatively small problem Islam presents in this area, let us consider it first. Our discussion will then turn to Buddhism, Hinduism, Judaism, Christianity, and Goddess Religion and Witchcraft.

ISLAM

Although in the course of its history, Islam has been influenced by debates such as that conducted in the ninth century by the Mu'tazilites regarding the use of human imagery for God, the religion largely remains loyal to its concept of the sovereign transcendence of Allah. Allah cannot be depicted in any tangible form. "No event or creature could stand for Allah sacramentally, as the rites or icons of other theisms could stand for their people's God."[1] Therefore, references regarding Allah as male do not have the same significance for Muslims as they seem to have for Jews and Christians considering God. According to the Islamic scholar Riffat Hassan, the fact that the pronoun used for Allah is male is more indicative of the Arabic genderization of words than of any masculine imaging of God.[2] Literature written by Muslim women supports this conclusion, in that such writings are greatly concerned with analyzing the place of women in Islam but have little if anything to say about images of God. The absence of such a concern is evidenced by one feminist, Sartaz Aziz, who writes,

> I am deeply grateful that my first ideas of God were formed by Islam because I was enabled to think of the Highest Power as one completely without sex or race, and thus completely unpatriarchal. . . . We begin with the ideal of a deity who is completely above sexual identity, and thus completely outside the value system created by patriarchy.[3]

That God is one, transcendent and beyond gender, is central to Islam. Even the concept of Messiah is anathema. According to Hassan, any imaging or assigning of gender to Allah for the purpose of becoming more closely identified to God is contrary to the experience of the Prophet and the early Muslims for whom "God was, indeed, closer than their jugular vein (see Qaf 50:16)."[4] Muslims, therefore, do not use a masculine God as either a conscious or unconscious tool in the construction of gender roles. What oppression does exist, therefore, originates in other sources.

BUDDHISM

Like Islamic women, the women in Buddhism are free of gender-specific images of the Godhead that Jewish and Christian feminists are bound to encounter. In fact, in recent years a growing number of American women have left their traditional Jewish and Christian roots to take up the Buddhist practice. Reasons for this phenomenon appear to be the non-dualistic, non-gendered nature of the Buddhist idea. Ellen Sidor, an editor of a collection by American Buddhist Teachers, believes that such women are attracted by the "Buddha's teaching of 'no discrimination.' "[5]

Although Buddhism has suffered the effects of the social and historical situations in which it developed, women practitioners maintain the initial non-dualistic nature of the dharma. Although this term in Sanskrit has a very wide meaning that includes the concepts of law, cosmic law of righteousness, religion and norm, it is used here to mean the truth, that which really is, that which makes up the components of ultimate reality.[6] In the introduction to her book, *Meetings With Remarkable Women*, Lenore Friedman writes, "the dharma itself is beyond ambivalence, resting nowhere, shattering concepts. The *teaching* of the dharma is another matter, since it arises from minds and from language conditioned by history and personal experience."[7] In the Mahayana tradition, the teaching of Emptiness is particularly appealing to those seeking a non-dualistic reality on which to base their existence. Because it is impossible to give any accurate description of the teaching in the space of our discussion, it must suffice to cite this short characterization from an introductory text on Buddhism by Richard Robinson:

> The perfection of wisdom consists in the direct realization that all the dharmas, whether conditioned or unconditioned, are empty. . . . Empty entities are neither existent nor inexistent. Either extreme would be heretical. . . . The teaching of emptiness repudiates dualities: between the conditioned and the unconditioned, between subject and object, between the pure and the impure, between the relative and the absolute. It cannot be called monism, however, because it denies that reality is either a plurality or a unity; it is simply beyond individuation and numbers, both of which are fictive concepts and mere designations.[8]

In his elaboration of the consequences of this doctrine, Robinson enumerates the powers of a bodhisattva or enlightened one. One of these special abilities is recognizing "the religious capacities of women, listening respectfully when they preach the Dharma, because he knows that maleness and femaleness are both empty."[9] Thus we can see that for a Buddhist, particularly a Mahayana Buddhist, the Ultimate Reality, whether you choose to call it the Dharma, Nirvana, or Emptiness, transcends gender; it is non-dualistic and beyond not only all sex differences but any other dichotomies as well.

HINDUISM

The Hindu concept of Brahman, too, contains the characteristic of being beyond duality. Without going into a history of Hindu philosophy, we must focus on this concept of Brahman, most basic to all Hindu thought. It is necessary to keep in mind, however, that Hinduism is perhaps the most difficult religion to summarize because it defies any simple explanation. It is unique among world religions because, in the words of Radhakrishnan,

> Hinduism is the religion not only of the Vedas but of the Epics and the Puranas. By accepting the significance of the different intuitions of reality and the different scriptures of the peoples living in India, Hinduism has come to be a tapestry of the most variegated tissues and almost endless diversity of hues. . . . Hinduism is therefore not a

definite dogmatic creed, but a vast, complex, but subtly unified mass of spiritual thought and realization.[10]

Once we acknowledge this fact, we cautiously proceed to examine the Ultimate Reality of Hinduism. It is the one religion which believes in an impersonal Ultimate Reality, Brahman, which at the same time has personal representations. It can claim to be monistic in that Brahman is one, yet contains a whole pantheon of gods and goddesses worshipped by the Hindu. What is this Brahman? It is an energy, a creative power which is at once outside of us and within us; it is transcendent omnipotence as well as immanent creativity. The definition of Heinrich Zimmer renders this complex term somewhat explicable. He writes,

> Brahman . . . is the crystallized, frozen form . . . of the highest divine energy. This energy is perennially latent in man, dormant, yet capable of being stirred to creative wakefulness through concentration . . . Brahman . . . is that through which we live and act, the fundamental spontaneity of our nature . . . Brahman . . . the highest, deepest, final, transcendental power inhabiting the visible, tangible levels of our nature, . . . cosmic power, in the supreme sense of the term, is the essence of all that we are and know. All things have been precipitated wonderfully out of its omnipresent all-transcending omnipotence.[11]

The Upanishads, in illuminating the meaning of Brahman, tell us that, while defying logical categories or linguistic symbols, Brahman is one self-subsistent reality. It is both qualityless (*nirguna* Brahman) and with qualities (*saguna* Brahman): both the incomprehensible pure absolute and the personal God who caused the world. Brahman is the source of all that is, the ground and dwelling place of selves.[12]

It is the *Brhadaranyaka Upanishad* which "has made famous the mystical doctrine of the indescribability of the Absolute."[13] It describes the unity of Brahman in IV.iv.20, which says

> As a unity only is It to be looked upon —
> This indemonstrable, enduring Being,
> Spotless, beyond space,
> The unborn Self, great, enduring.[14]

Again in IV.v.15 we read "That Self (*Atman*) is not this, it is not that [this] (*neti,neti*). It is unseizable, for it cannot be seized; indestructible, for it cannot be destroyed; unattached, for it does not attach itself; is unbound, does not tremble, is not injured . . ."[15]

According to Radhakrishnan, there are different notions of God in Hinduism that are not distinguished as true and false but that are rather seen as stages one must go through in order to arrive at ultimate reality. He understands the bewildering polytheism of the masses and the uncompromising monotheism of the sages as expressions of one and the same force at different levels. The thinking Hindu desires to escape from the confusion of the gods into the silence of the Supreme, while the crowd still stands gazing at the heavens.[16]

This concept of levels gives an explanation to the varied forms of worship of personal gods and goddesses among Hindus. David Kinsley, however, holds a different explanation. He views the huge diversity of the Hindu pantheon as testifying to the fact that for the Hindu the divine cannot be circumscribed. The idea of a divinity rather excites the imagination to incredible and even extreme lengths in an attempt to understand the world in its fullness.[17]

Whether one views the personal gods and goddesses in Hinduism as part of a lower stage of spiritual development or as an exciting form of the divine realization, it is evident that the formless Brahman when taking on forms takes them on as both male and female. And this is the significant point for us in examining the Hindu contribution to the philosophy of religion from a feminist perspective. While feminine representations of the deity can take on a myriad of interpretations in Hinduism, the mere fact that they exist stands as a reminder that feminine power must be reckoned with in some way. It cannot be ignored or completely subsumed under a male guise.

JUDAISM

The story is quite different, however, when we turn to the monotheistic religions of Judaism and Christianity. Both of these traditions have adhered to deeply embedded male images of the divine reality. Believing that this imagery has served to bring about and support much of the androcentrism and misogyny in these religions, feminists have critiqued the concepts of God and the language used to communicate these concepts.

That this critique is vital to a renewal of Judaism is adamantly expressed by some Jewish feminists. Susannah Heschel, for one, believes that the feminist inquiry challenges the very basis of Judaism from *halakhah* (unwritten law) to the prayer book to the very ways in which we conceive of God. A new theology of Judaism is emerging, requiring that we come to new understandings of God. As long as God is father and king in Jewish theology, claims Heschel, women will always stand as other while men are the true subjects.[18]

To illustrate the work being done by Jewish feminists in the philosophy of religion, there is a wonderful account of a group of Jewish women who meet regularly to discuss the meaning of being both female and Jewish. The initial difficulties of this group are recounted in the Fall 1986 issue of the *Journal of Feminist Studies in Religion*. Some of their differences were strongly felt when the group attempted to engage in *davvening* (communal prayer). After some members experienced anger, and others elation, they worked together to achieve a form that all could be comfortable with. One description of the result is as follows:

> We have experimented with *davvening* in the context of casting a circle; we have *davvened* the traditional liturgy (feminizing the name of God/dess); and we have used entirely new liturgies and images, but incorporating a nonsexist, nonhierarchical view of God and Israel. None of these transitions has been easy. Though we knew we wanted to pray in a feminist way, to a feminist God, we realized that we imaged the God we did (or could) pray to in very different ways.[19]

Although many Jewish feminists are insisting on the use of female language and imagery for God, others also realize that using these terms could convey God "as passive and receptive. Instead, [these] feminists suggest strong, dynamic, creative, and active images of the female."[20] Thus we have a double problem when trying to portray the divine or attempting to answer the question of the nature of the divine. Not only do we need to examine the words used to express the divine essence, but we must also examine the connotations and traditional meanings of these words. In other words, a thorough linguistic analysis is called for when attempting to speak of the Jewish concept of Ultimate Reality.

CHRISTIANITY

Many feminist scholars have emerged within the Christian tradition and have taken up the philosophical question concerning the nature of the divine. They have critiqued the Christian concept of God as patriarchal and paternalistic. These women are examining the meaning of the images and symbols used for God in Christianity and the expression of the experience of Ultimate Reality or the dimension of transcendence.

A major stress in the study of the male images, symbols, and metaphors for the divine has been to examine the very nature of these images, symbols, and metaphors themselves. How well do these terms represent the Ultimate Reality? What are the dangers of using them in a religious context? An analysis of these questions is part of the extensive study done by Sallie McFague in her work, *Metaphorical Theology: Models of God in Religious Language*. One of her main points is that Christians tend to use the language of metaphor, language that only partially can represent the transcendent, as language that identifies God. She writes that religious language "becomes *idolatrous* because without a sense of awe, wonder, and mystery, we forget the inevitable distance between our words and the divine reality."[21] According to McFague, metaphorical theology understands that true images need not be literal and meaningful images need not be traditional.[22] The images of father, and the metaphor of overseer and parent, have been so pervasive in Christianity that the terms themselves have become sacred. The conclusion of this observation could be that Christians are unwilling to change the image for one that is perhaps richer because they see the traditional one as literally true.

Rosemary Ruether echoes the work of McFague in her book *Sexism and God-Talk*. In it she writes,"the proscription of idolatry must . . . be extended to verbal pictures. When the word *Father* is taken literally to mean that God is male and not female, represented by males and not females then this word becomes idolatrous."[23] Although Christian doctrine teaches that all language referring to God is analogy and that God is both male and female and neither male nor female, the exclusive use of male terms has resulted nevertheless in the literal and idolatrous understanding of a male God. Therefore, according to Ruether, "one needs inclusive language for God that draws on the images and experiences of both genders. Inclusiveness can happen only by naming God/ess in female as well as male metaphors."[24]

Not only does Ruether object to the use of the metaphor "father" for God on grounds that this is a sexist term, but also on grounds that the whole idea of parent leaves Christians with a very parental view of God who encourages their behavior as children.

> Parent model for the divine has negative resonances. . . . It suggests a kind of permanent parent-child relationship to God. . . . Patriarchal theology uses the parent image for God to prolong spiritual infantilism as virtue and to make autonomy and assertion of free will a sin. Parenting in patriarchal society also becomes the way of enculturating us to the stereotypic male and female roles.[25]

Remembering that God can never be accurately imaged and that our words can only be feeble communicators of the divine reality, we must understand "parent" as an image of God and not God in itself. If we did confine a definition of God to parent, would we not be falling into the very same idolatrous trap that McFague warns us against?

The conclusion of these sections of the work of Ruether and McFague is that the language that we use to talk about God is replete with significance. The fact that Christian doctrine maintains the inexpressibility of God's nature is not sufficient justification to ignore the dangers of using sexist language. Language conjures up metaphors and images. Metaphors and images compose our conceptual framework that, in turn, influences our faith and values. Hence exclusive language for God has a great bearing on who and what Christians believe the Ultimate Reality to be, and, in the past, Christians have believed this Ultimate Reality to be male.

No one has pointed to the significance of language used for God quite as forcibly as Mary Daly. In *Beyond God the Father*, she succinctly states the problem: "If God is male, then male is God."[26] Because Christians have used masculine images for god, then "men have godlike attributes."[27] While this leap may appear unjustified, McFague argues its validity with two points. First, she underscores the dominance of such imagery as lord, judge, father, king, and master in the Christian tradition. Second, she emphasizes the interactive character of models, that is, the way in which the model and the modeled mutually influence each other. Therefore, if the male models God, then God also models the man.[28]

With so much import given to the use of male images when talking about the divine, one can understand why women philosophers and theologians are sensitive to language. One can also understand why it would be difficult for a Jewish or Christian woman to engage in interreligious dialogue with male counterparts who use such images. In these situations, some very rudimentary issues of the nature of the Godhead have either not been dealt with or, if they have, are in complete opposition to those views held by the feminist. In either case, a major obstacle to dialogue exists.

Then what is the feminist solution to male images of God? Should we substitute female images? If we do, we run into a dilemma similar to that confronted by the Jewish feminists spoken of earlier: that is, female images will carry with them the feminine side of the very same dualism that Christian feminists are trying to overcome. Ursula King explains that "the replacement of the patriarchal god-symbol by the counter-symbol of the goddess does not overcome the fundamental dualism underlying patriarchy but merely replaces it by its opposite."[29] Even the attempt to put both the female and male images together to form a type of androgyne fails to serve the feminist purpose. The very real problem that exists with the idea of an androgynous God is that the concept presupposes a psychic dualism that identifies maleness with one half of human capacities and femaleness with the other half. In the opinion of Rosemary Ruether, androgyny, whether it identifies woman with the lower material nature or with the higher spiritual qualities of altruistic love, never succeeds in allowing woman to represent full human potential.[30]

What can be done? How do we get out of the bind of gender-identifying traits of God and come up with an image that is both gender neutral and gender inclusive? Ruether poses one possible image as a solution—that of God/ess as Matrix, which we look upon not as parent, but as source and ground of our being. Understanding that feminist philosophy and theology must reject the matter/spirit dualism, Ruether envisions a

God/ess who is the foundation (at one and the same time) of our being and our new being embraces both the roots of the material substratum of our existence (matter) and also the endlessly new creative potential (spirit). The God/ess who is the foundation of our being-new being does not lead us back to a stifled, dependent self or uproot us in a spirit-trip outside the earth. Rather it leads us to the converted center, the harmonization of self and body, self and other, self and world. It is the *Shalom* of our being.[31]

GODDESS RELIGION AND WITCHCRAFT

The feminist scholars mentioned above represent only a few of the many women who have chosen to speculate on the nature of the divine while remaining within their respective religious traditions. They challenge the existing images and symbols and yet attempt to create new ones that may speak to persons who wish to continue to be a part of historical religions.

There are some women scholars and practitioners of religion, however, who find the systems of tradition beyond repair. The only way they can understand themselves as being religious persons is by separating from the past and formulating a new tradition in which their relationship with the Ultimate Reality can flourish. Mary Daly, in an essay first published in 1971, wrote that

The women's movement will present a growing threat to patriarchal religion less by attacking it than by simply leaving it behind ... For the present, it would appear that we are being called upon to recognize the poverty of all symbols and the fact of our past idolatry regarding them, and to turn to our own resources for bringing about the radically new in our own lives.[32]

And, as if to follow her advice, some feminists have done just that. They found new symbols and new expressions that have now grown into new religions, specifically called the Goddess Religion and the Wicca Movement.

Goddess spirituality, writes Merlin Stone, arose out of the "emerging interest in the history and prehistory of ancient cultures that worshipped a female deity."[33] Stone found that "the development of the religion of the female deity ... was intertwined with the earliest beginnings of religion so far discovered anywhere on earth."[34] Feminists are returning to those roots to rediscover the nature of a deity that existed prior to its definition by men holding a patriarchal and misogynistic world view.

Carol Christ, one of the foremost proponents of Goddess religion, rejected Christianity because, although for her the biblical concept of God was "beyond sexuality," as theological tradition asserts, there remained a certain aura of masculine presence and authority.[35] She claims that in order for woman to see herself in the image of this biblical God she would have to deny her own sexual identity.[36] Therefore, by finding a new image of God in the Goddess, she is able to acknowledge not only her sexual identity but also the "legitimacy of female power as a beneficent and independent power."[37]

But what is the meaning of the Goddess? Is the word simply another name for God, representing another single-sex system? Christ insists that it is not and illustrates her point by elaborating on the different meanings that feminists have given the term. In *Laughter of Aphrodite*, she speaks of women who have used the term as a new name for ultimate power or powers.[38] Others have discovered that it is a very old name and are reclaiming its ancient meaning. Goddess has been used to signify an energy that is fundamental and universal. It is an energy that causes the natural processes of life and death, attraction and repulsion, as well as that concentrated in meditation, ritual, and psychic healing.

Christ, herself, sees the Goddess from a Christian perspective and through Tillich's influence. For her, the Goddess gave life to the abstract idea of Ground of Being, and has great meaning as her image of the divinity. "Not until I said *Goddess* did I realize that I had never felt fully included in the fullness of my being as *woman* in masculine or neuterized imagery for divinity."[39]

However the symbol of Goddess is used, whether to express one divine reality or one aspect of an ultimately plural reality, the very use of the term in Western religious consciousness is part of a widespread grassroots movement of women's spirituality that has emerged spontaneously in the United States and elsewhere.

According to Charlene Spretnak, the Goddess image has gained great popularity among feminists because it offers a more holistic anthropomorphized concept of the deity:

> She is *immanent* in our lives and our world . . . She contains both female and male, in Her womb, as a male deity cannot; all beings are *part of Her*, not distant creations. She also symbolizes the power of the female body /mind. There is no "party line" of Goddess worship; rather, each person's process of perceiving and living Her truth is a movement in the larger dance—hence the phrase "The Goddess is All."[40]

These feminists believe that by worshipping the Goddess, a woman is acknowledging that the divine principle, the saving and sustaining power, is in herself: she need no longer view men or male figures as saviors.

One specific form that the Goddess religion has taken is Witchcraft. Starhawk, a witch who has written much about the movement—or in her terms, "The Craft"—says that "Goddess religion is unimaginably old, but contemporary Witchcraft could just as accurately be called the New Religion. The Craft, today, . . . is experiencing a renaissance, a re-creation."[41] Because witches understand the world as a manifestation of the Goddess, Witchcraft can be seen as a "religion of ecology. Its goal is harmony with nature, so that life may not just survive, but thrive."[42] For witches, the Goddess is an immanent reality that, while manifested in nature, is still in need of "human help to realize Her fullest beauty."[43] This movement is not to be misunderstood as simply conservation or even as pantheism. It is a religion with communities (covens), rituals, and ethical standards; it does not involve merely passive worship of nature. Craft rituals aim at renewing the harmonious balance of nature and include not only meditations but also "cleaning up garbage left at a campsite or marching to protest an unsafe nuclear plant."[44]

Perhaps the most striking aspect of Witchcraft as a form of Goddess religion is that it has taken the idea of a feminine image of the Divine Reality and given it an exclusively immanent definition. By doing so, it has enhanced the sense of personal power that Carol Christ spoke of in her image of female deity. Starhawk describes the essence of this sense of personal power in the following passage from her work, *Truth or Dare.*

> The Goddess, the Gods, the great powers, are the material world, are us. If they extend beyond us they do so like the sun's corona flaring beyond its core. No power is entirely separate from our own power, no being is entirely separate from our own being.[45]

In sum, the branch of Goddess religion called Witchcraft releases women and men from the strife of dualisms, from war between the spiritual and the material. It allows us to

> open new eyes and see that there is nothing to be saved *from*, no struggle of life *against* the universe, no God outside the world to be feared and obeyed; only the Goddess, the Mother, the turning spiral that whirls us in and out of existence.[46]

CONCLUSION

What are the implications of these observations for interreligious dialogue? After reviewing the concepts of God held by feminists in the diversity of religions, we realize that these women would encounter a problem holding discussions with men who used gender specific images for the deity. The women from traditions in which the Ultimate transcended sexuality are finding it necessary to stress this point in order to ward off the cultural and societal male dominance that has found its way into religious practice. These women would be at odds with men of all traditions who accepted, either actively or passively, the exclusive use of male references for this deity.

Jewish and Christian women, especially, would have a greater problem with their male colleagues. Unless the male representatives of the monotheistic faiths were able to view the oppressive significance of the traditional male images of God (and not dismiss the issue as *merely* language), dialogue could not be fruitful. So far in most of the interreligious dialogue among predominantly male participants, God has rarely if ever been referred to in gender inclusive language. Men have continually referred to God as "He" without considering any of the philosophical and theological works of which the above descriptions are only a sampling.

Another serious consideration here involves the ramifications for a discussion of women among themselves. If Buddhist, Hindu, and to some extent Muslim women see the object of their traditions as being gender neutral or transcending sex differences, there will be a problem. Their Jewish and Christian sisters are working hard to counteract the thousands of years of imaging God as male by presenting a more complete picture. In so doing, not only are they reimaging God but also changing the meaning of being female. The Jewish and Christian women are not interested in doing away with sex differences but rather enhancing the meaning of sexuality and placing it in a context of spirituality. While the Mahayana and Vendanta sisters do not see sex as a philosophical problem, because they are called to transcend these differences, the Jewish and Christian sisters are trying to find ways to live consciously in their sexual situations and still participate fully in their religious traditions.

If these differences exist among women within the historical religious traditions, how much greater and more complicated will be the differences when followers of the Goddess and of Witchcraft enter into the discussion. These women usually do not wish to transcend sexuality, but in fact see their identity as female sexual beings at the locus of reality. Working all these perspectives into some kind of mutually enriching dialogue will be the intent of the following pages.

5

Communication Theory

Up to this point we have examined the philosophical and theological reasons why women have been excluded from the major work in interreligious dialogue. We have studied the content of the dialogue and some of the philosophical concepts upon which it is based.

In this section, we turn to an area that involves not so much the content but the method of dialogue itself—communication. It is necessary to examine communication theory because very often the manner in which people speak reveals more about their thoughts than do their words. If a lover proclaims her love without ever looking in the eyes of the beloved, the two probably shouldn't make wedding plans yet. If a male professor says that he is all for the equality of women, yet fails to listen to his female students' comments, he is probably a closet chauvinist. By studying the implications of how people talk and listen to one another, we will perhaps better understand why women have been excluded from interreligious dialogue.

RESEARCH IN THE FIELD OF COMMUNICATION

Communication theory consists of two aspects: (1) the study of language and (2) the way in which people communicate using this language. Recently, much research has explored gender issues in these areas. The findings, I believe, are not only very interesting but also very revealing for the process of interreligious dialogue, for this process is so dependent on verbal communication.

The very definition of gender itself is linked to language usage. One researcher, Lana Rakow, holds the opinion that gender and language are interdependent.

Our particular gender system of two dimorphic and asymmetrical genders is one of only a variety of systems that could be structured. It is in communication that this gender system is accomplished. Gender has meaning, is organized and structured and takes place as interaction and social practice, all of which are communication processes. That is, communication creates genders who create communication.[1]

Communication research, when linked with work in philosophy, psychology and anthropology, enables us to understand that gender is not a fixed unchangeable reality and that we cannot rely on any preconception of the nature of gender. Once this concept is grasped, we can begin to explore how our perceptions have affected communication as well as the role that communication has played in our perceptions. In their thorough study of the issue, Barbara and R. Gene Eakins have noted that "Whether the causes are cultural or genetic, sex differences in communication behavior are real."[2]

Our perceptions have affected communication. As a result, the way we communicate and the language we use reflect our world view and that of society as well. For example, the use of the title *Ms.* to replace *Mrs.* or *Miss* was an attempt by women to correct the traditional belief that a woman's marital status or her relationship to a man was one of the most important things about her, if not *the* most important, whereas a man's marital status was irrelevant.[3] Although people objected to its use on the grounds that they didn't know how to pronounce *Ms.*, the real issue was the rejection of a new set of beliefs about equal sex roles in our society.

Gender researchers have discovered that language is especially faithful in revealing social attitudes about male and female roles. To these researchers, language structure represents a social structure, not an abstract system of lexicon and grammar. By studying language, we can study the social enactment of relationships between women and men, the hierarchical organization of speakers, and linguistic strategies used to maintain one group's superiority.[4] Linguistic scholars further insist that, in the past, language has been produced and changed more by men than by women.[5]

Examination of the social constructs of language also reveals that language not only reflects the social attitudes and processes, but is a part of them and, even more importantly, helps shape them. Cheris Kramarae, the author of *Women and Speaking,* believes that "speech is always socially situated behavior, a part of social reality, not merely a reflection of it."[6] Eakins and Eakins seem to be echoing Kramarae when they write that "Language does not so much *reflect* society as it makes up a part of social process."[7]

Feminists have raised questions about this aspect of language and communication because, if it does influence the social structure, then there are major concerns about the ways in which language contributes to the construction of a male supremacist society.[8]

Whether the issue is one of language reflecting or of language influencing social attitudes, the fact remains that a study of language reveals male dominance and control. After extensive study, Eakins and Eakins found that the research in all areas of human communication consistently underscores the dominant power status of males and the dominated, subordinate status of females.[9] These results have also been found in languages other than English. Kramarae recounts a Norwegian study done by the researcher Rolv Mikkel Blakkar that demonstrates how language in different ways *reflects* and *conserves* the existing sex-role patterns. Further, it has been shown how boys and girls, both directly and indirectly, learn their traditional sex roles as they learn and understand their mother tongue.[10]

Many theorists support the idea that language is closely connected to the stereotypes of male and female role distinctions and to the value judgments placed on them. These theorists reason that because men and women have been conditioned to think and act in different ways, they communicate differently; this communication, in turn, reinforces the ways in which people view one another, thus confirming the stereotypes. In their study of stereotypes, Deborah Borisoff and Lisa Merrill found that men have been taught to be objective and impersonal, whereas women have been encouraged to be subjective and self-disclosing. Women make themselves vulnerable by their self-disclosure; men, by contrast, derive power from sounding authoritative and communicating facts rather than emotions. The positive male model of speaker is a person who is *"direct, confrontative, forceful and logical; whose few, well-chosen words are focused on making a particular point."*[11] These authors also report what has been known as the "double bind" for women. From early childhood, women have been taught to behave in certain ways. Robin Lakoff explains how they are "encouraged to be 'little ladies.' "[12] However, it is exactly this conditioning that forbids a woman to use strong language or to "bellow in rage."[13] Hence, she appears weak and superficial. As Borisoff and Merrill conclude,

> Consequently, the stereotype of the female speaker as insecure, superficial, and weak becomes self-perpetuating. Having been historically discouraged from speaking, women internalize the stereotype and fear violating the norm. This fear leads to the acculturated adoption of communicative strategies that . . . are the tactics of less powerful individuals, and when women adopt them, which they overwhelmingly do regardless of socio-economic stature, the perception of women's relative weakness as communicators is confirmed.[14]

Because men have been the dominant and stronger sex in society, they have structured and formed the language and have dominated verbal communication, rendering women mute. While this statement appears to be a broad indictment of men, these conclusions are actually drawn from empirical studies conducted in the field of language and communication. To repeat a former point, if we consider dialogue as consisting of language and communication, ought we not to examine it more closely and ask whether or not these same gender issues of male dominance and female stereotyping might apply to it as well?

Language involves a power issue, and studies indicate how men have exercised their power a great deal in this area.[15] The symbolic system of language was formed by men to explain the experiences of men; therefore, men have created the definitions and roles that are attached to gender. Lena Rakow cites studies done by Dale Spender which conclude that the "men have been able to structure and name a world that is amenable to their experiences and outlooks. Women and women's experiences have been negated and devalued as a result."[16] Men's words and not women's are listened to because men have provided the images and symbols in which thought is expressed and ordered.

After reading these women's findings, the message rings clearly. However, let one last citation summarize and leave no doubt that communication has been genderized. Eakins and Eakins also speak of power used in and by language:

> The power of naming or labeling has become a significant issue for the sexes. Those with the most power in our society will, consciously or unconsciously, cast their words in the forms most appropriate for them. The language of the favored group is generally accepted and used by those who are less powerful. Through naming, men have defined women's actions, attributes, ideas and very being in their own male terms.[17]

At this point in our discussion it becomes necessary to bring up a much belittled point regarding language: that of the use of the male pronouns, *he, him* or *his,* to refer to both men and women in a generic sense. Invariably when the subject is mentioned to those who do not use inclusive language, they consider the issue unimportant and trivial. Indeed, as the linguist Wendy Martyna realized, even some feminists "consider the fight for 'equal words' to be misdirection of energy."[18] She theorizes that the resistance to change is not simply the resistance to feminism but also "a general cultural reluctance to acknowledge the power of language in our lives, an insistence that language is of symbolic rather than actual importance."[19] Martyna notes that "research has begun to suggest the behavioral implications of sexist language. . . . The data on the way the generic *he* encourages a male rather than a neutral interpretation . . . is considerable."[20] Thorne, Kramarae and Henley report that

> there is ample research evidence that the masculine "generic" does not really function as a generic. In various studies words like *he* and *man* in generic contexts were presented orally or in writing to people who were asked to indicate their understanding by drawing, bringing in, or pointing out a picture, by describing or writing a story about the person(s) referred to, or by answering yes or no when asked whether a sex-specific word or picture applies to the meaning. . . . In

all of these studies women and girls were understood to be included significantly less often than men and boys, a finding true for both female and male subjects ... both women and men report that they usually image males when they read or hear the masculine "generic."[21]

Eakins and Eakins devote a section of their text, *Sex Differences in Human Communication*, to these studies, and they report that "Linguists have analyzed and categorized the ways in which generic language subsumes and renders women invisible."[22] After listing and discussing these ways, they conclude that "although language experts may declare that generic terms refer to women by implication, the *interpretation* of them may be biased toward the male."[23]

SEXIST LANGUAGE IN DIALOGUE

Taking all of these findings into consideration, we will draw attention now to some examples of the use of sexist language in interreligious dialogue. The book *The Myth of Christian Uniqueness* is a collection of published versions of papers that were discussed at a conference held in Claremont, California in 1986. One of these papers, written by Raimundo Panikkar, contains the sentence, "The Christian is the Man of *faith.*"[24] Evidently the editors wished to change the phrase but were not permitted to do so. Instead they placed an asterisk after the word "Man" and referred the reader to the following footnote:

> Editor's Note: Dr. Panikkar has requested that the editors keep his particular usage of "Man." He explains: "Neither *purusa*, nor *anthropos*, nor *homo* ... , nor *Mensch* ... nor analagous words in other cultures, stand for the male alone. I would not want to give males the monopoly on humanness (from *homo*) nor would I want to contribute to the fragmentation of 'Man' (the knower) by accepting the fragmentation of knowledge when dealing with that being which stands between heaven and earth and, different from other entities, knows it. No discrimination! As I have explained elsewhere, 'wo-man' can be a derogatory expression, for it betrays male domination (and 'feminine' submission)."[25]

A number of issues are involved in Panikkar's note; but, in light of the present discussion, just a few are pressing. First, he seems to be implying that if one word is inclusive and signifies both male and female in other languages, then the same meaning ought to be true for the English word as well. However, Panikkar seems to be ignoring the distinction between a literal translation and a more connotative one. The English word *man* may be a direct translation of *Mensch* and *anthropos*, but while the words can be carried over, the meaning cannot. The situation is parallel to that of the

Greek word *sarx*, which is translated literally as "flesh" and appears often in St. Paul's epistles. Exegetes have determined that Paul did not mean what the English word conveys, that is, bodily tissue. Thus newer translations have had to find more accurate English words to substitute, one of which is *self-indulgence*. I suggest, therefore, that if *mensch* and *anthropos* cannot be accurately translated by the English word *man*, which is exclusive and connotes males only, then it should be changed to *humanity* or *person*. In using other languages to justify the use of the word *man*, Panikkar ignores the finer points of translation so necessary to remain faithful to a text.

Second, Panikkar believes that the use of another word for man — such as *person* or *human* — would "fragment . . . that being which stands between heaven and earth." How does the division by sex fragment the knowing being? My sense is that either Panikkar is ignoring the two equal ways of being human, or he believes that woman cannot be knower in the same sense that man is, and, therefore, mention of her would detract from that being "who stands between heaven and earth." Either way, woman is the loser: either her existence is not acknowledged or she is subsumed under the male of the species. Simply stating that he does not "want to give man the monopoly on humanness" does not in fact prove that he doesn't. The third and final comment refers to Panikkar's last remark that " 'wo-man' can be a derogatory expression, for it betrays male domination. . . . " Precisely the point, and by Panikkar's refusal to use the symbol for woman in his sentence "The Christian is the Man of faith," he is perpetuating and reinforcing exactly what he wishes to escape.

There were several other instances in this text where the published version of the papers contained inclusive language, whereas the drafts that were distributed at the conference did not. Many of the original works did contain sexist language; in fact, sexist language was used in the dialogue far more than in the publication of the works.

COMMUNICATION TECHNIQUES AND DIALOGUE

Besides being concerned with the language itself, researchers are also examining communication techniques. There are very significant differences found in the way men and women communicate, both in same-sex groups and in mixed-sex groups. Kramarae quotes the findings of a study conducted by Edwin Ardener in 1975. Ardener concluded that "groups that are on top of the social hierarchy determine to a great extent the dominant communication system of a society. Subordinate groups (such as children and women) are made 'inarticulate.' "[26] This result, coupled with her own findings, has led Kramarae to develop the muted-group theory. Because women's perceptions differ from those of men, and the words and norms for speaking are not fitted to women's experiences, women are "muted." Their talk is often not considered of much value by men who are, or who appear to be, deaf and blind to much of women's experiences. Words that are constantly ignored eventually come to be unspoken and perhaps even unthought.[27]

One of the consequences of this theory is that women are, for the most part, not heard in the public forum. Interreligious dialogue takes place in a public forum. Can we apply the muted-group theory to this arena? Looking at Kramarae's words more closely, we find the following in her introduction to *Women and Men Speaking*:

> Women who speak publicly and to audiences that include men experience particular difficulties. ... My historical survey of women's efforts to speak in public (Kramarae, 1978) reveals that their public presence has been tolerated at times when their speech was not. ... Although women do not encounter hostility in all public speaking situations, women's public speech is especially restricted when women wish to address mixed-sex or male adult audiences, and when women attempt to speak on issues and in places considered important to men.[28]

Religious and philosophical principles are "considered important to men," and a degree of involvement occurs when these subjects are discussed. If this be the case, doesn't interreligious dialogue present a situation to which Kramarae's theory would apply?

Another aspect of communication in interreligious dialogue—to be detailed later—concerns the way the dialogue is organized. Communication theorists have found that gender plays a role in how public speaking is conducted. Perhaps there is an application here as well.

The traditional gender roles of Western society have contributed to the fact that males gravitate towards participating in public speeches and debates, whereas women are encouraged to listen. In other words, organized public speeches represent a value whereas mediation and quiet listening takes secondary importance. This, unfortunately, seems to be the dominant view so that when women deviate from this male norm by refusing to conduct business with organized speeches or step out of their assigned female role by speaking up forcefully instead of acquiescing, they are often not heard.

Some further consequences of the muted group theory are the following: (1) that "women and their concerns continue to be of marginal importance in men's perception,"[29] (2) that "males have more difficulty than females in understanding what members of the other gender mean,"[30] and (3) that "men suffer and cause others to suffer, from an inability or unwillingness to self-disclose, to discuss feelings, and to do interaction support work."[31]

Examples of these consequences can be found in the academic arena, in philosophy and theology conferences, and at interreligious dialogues. A particular instance occurred at a conference in Claremont, California, on the subject of the debate between realism and non-realism in the philosophy of religion. Of the eighteen participants, two were women. One of the women gave a formal response to a paper in which she called for the disclosure of the personal experience of faith insofar as that would shed light on one's philosophical position. She asked if "it is possible, at a conference like this, for us to gain insight further and faster by laying out in narrative form our own personal trajectories, by giving emphasis to the intellectual and other prominent influences that mark our life stories."[32] She was a woman raising a question not commonly raised by men in academic dialogue. After her remarks were delivered, one participant thanked her for an excellent presentation and proceeded to respond to an earlier comment made by a male colleague. The woman's remarks were never brought up again. Later in the concluding remarks, when comments from the observers were entertained, a member of the audience took note of the omissions by the group, indicating that the neglect by the male participants was obvious, not only to the woman who gave the response but to the observers as well.

This example illustrates two of the above points regarding the muted-group theory: (1) self-disclosure is not part of the male-constituted tools of expression and (2) since the concern of the presentation was expressed by a woman and labeled as such, it was not considered important by the male colleagues. My purpose is not to examine the specific motivations of the individual members of this particular conference; it is, rather, to point to the phenomenon in the area of philosophy and suggest how it might be interpreted in light of modern communication theory.

If these hypotheses are true, then what have we learned? If communication styles are so very different and language is understood differently by men and women, then women need first to talk among themselves. Only then will they have the assurance of being heard, and, because their language and style of communication is understood, real dialogue can take place.

But is this all? Are we doomed to separatism? I suggest that there *is* hope for mutual understanding and communication between the sexes, but there are certain tasks to be accomplished before this is realized. First, different roles must be valued for themselves and divorced from their association with one sex. A wide range of behaviors needs to be accepted for both genders.

Second, changes are required for the improvement of communication between sexes. Changes are possible for both men and women. I suggest, however, that until these attitudinal changes occur, women must be heard in same-sex circles. They must begin to experience the speaking and listening that will give them voice and end the period of mutedness so long endured. In the future, we must develop new ways to communicate that will facilitate greater understanding between men and women, particularly in the area of interreligious dialogue.

PART II

Problems Unique
to Women's Dialogue

6

The Universality of Feminism

Much dialogue among women concerns the experience of oppression in both social and religious contexts. However, the fact that the issue of oppression is an integral part of women's dialogue poses a problem that must be addressed before any dialogue can be productive. This problem stems from the variety of answers to a significant question: are all women throughout the world working to eliminate a conscious experience of oppression? In other words, is feminism a universal phenomenon? Because oppression is a socio-political issue, it is important to understand the crucial relationship in women's dialogue between religious beliefs and the socio-political situation.

RELIGION AND THE SOCIAL CONDITION

In current interreligious dialogues, participants are becoming increasingly aware of the need to explore ways in which abstract religious beliefs both affect and are affected by the social situations in which the religions are practiced. Several participants have suggested ways in which the topics of justice and political praxis can offer a common ground for dialogue and therefore be a more unifying alternative to the discussion of conflicting truth claims. For women, however, the discussion of practical social aspects of religion is not simply a more desirable alternative but an absolute necessity. Such a discussion of religion will deal with some aspect of women's place in the society, be it oppressive or liberating. In other words, to talk about religion is to talk about women's lived experience.

Increasingly, male theologians engaged in dialogue understand the need to talk about the social situation. This need is felt because there has been a growing awareness of the impact of religion on even the most secular of societies. Christian liberation theology has contributed greatly to this awareness, both of theologians as a whole and of dialogue participants in particular. Paul Knitter describes the effects of this movement in an essay in his collection *The Myth of Christian Uniqueness*. He writes that "from the perspective of those concerned with liberation, the past decade has indicated what an important and powerful role religion can play, for better or for worse, in bringing about socio-political transformation."[1] Knitter goes so far as to say that "theologians engaged in dialogue are realizing that religion that does not address, as a primary concern, the poverty and oppression that infest our world is not authentic religion. . . . Something essential is missing in . . . other-worldly or ultra-academic dialogue."[2]

Leonard Swidler, in his recent study of interreligious dialogue, offers a similar viewpoint. He writes that "religions and ideologies are not only explanations of the meaning of life, but also ways . . . to live according to that explanation."[3] Both of these theologians put forth the idea that the goal and purpose of dialogue with other religions is and should be, as Swidler writes, "joint [social] action on . . . concrete problems."[4] In Knitter's words, "We go out to meet others . . . to eliminate suffering and oppression . . . to work for justice. Justice . . . takes precedence over pluralism, dialogue and even charity."[5] While neither Swidler nor Knitter speaks of the liberation of women explicitly, this issue may be implied in several references in their works. Knitter, for example, writes about the *"preferential option for the poor and the nonperson* [constituting] the *primary purpose of dialogue."*[6] If the non-person has been understood to be all those who have not been recognized in their full stature as persons while still being able to subsist economically, then perhaps women fall into this category.

Meanwhile, as these two theologians work to convince a male-dominated dialogue group to move towards a more justice-oriented discussion, many women who have begun dialogue with a secular concept of justice as their major concern have begun to discuss religion. Women are beginning to realize that religion is an essential part in their discussions of social structures and oppression. They recognize that if transformation is to take place, religion must be considered. In sum, men are seeing that religion can't be adequately discussed unless it is in the context of social realities. Women, on the other hand, are realizing that oppression and justice can't be adequately analyzed and changed without giving due consideration to religion.

An example of this new awareness on the part of women occurred at the Conference in Nairobi, Kenya, that closed the U.N. Decade for Women in 1985. A Protestant minister attending the conference noted that, for the first time, the subjects of religion and religious practice were part of the forum and the women's questions were more and more concerned with religious issues.[7] Of course, in explicitly religious environments like that of the Harvard Divinity School, this connection between the oppression of women and religion had been explored much earlier. In 1983, a conference was organized by Diana Eck and Devaki Jain for just such exploration. Eck and Jain were convinced that "In both its progressive and reactionary forms, religion has entered into and shaped almost every major conflict and crisis in the world today."[8] Hence, the question posed to the conference participants was, "What is the relation of religion to the kinds of social change projects and struggles in which women are engaged around the world?"[9] The results are complex and revealing, but at this point the issue being considered is that, for women, as for other people seeking liberation, there is a vital connection between social justice and religion. This connection demands that a discussion of one includes a discussion of the other.

Considering this connection between social norms and religion, it is logical to conclude that if women wish to change their social status, they must develop a new theology and realize the implications behind the religious underpinnings of society. Along with Eck and Jain, so many women are realizing that an understanding of religious issues is basic to changing the situation of women. A culture's religious traditions *are* its basis for meaning-making, image-making, and creating an ordered world and an ethos. However, religious images, including images of women, have been created by men and have been, for the culture as a whole, even for "secular" participants in culture, profoundly influential in determining attitudes toward women.[10]

When women do not appreciate this interconnectedness, their work for change becomes ineffective. If the women who are investigating feminist theology and philosophy do not recognize what they share with their political counterparts, then their efforts remain irrelevant. By the same token, the fight for women's rights in the secular arena will be weakened if it fails to acknowledge the religious dimension of the problem. The feminist philosopher Charlotte Bunch noted that culture and spirit are integral parts of all movements for change. A polarization of these realms is disastrous for feminism.[11] Scholars and activists alike are recognizing that religion can be a powerful agent of social transformation. They have observed that religion, more than any other force, is able to release enormous bursts of energy that are necessary to alter the directions of peoples and nations.[12]

IS FEMINISM UNIVERSAL?

Understanding that talk of religion and talk of social change cannot be separate issues in dialogue among women, we encounter some problems that such a dialogue entails. When social oppressions are discussed, a group cannot naively search for some abstract Ultimate Reality held in common by all participants. Instead, specific social situations must be confronted, cultural diversity acknowledged, and the haze of myriad experiences analyzed.

The issue of feminism is essential to any interreligious and intercultural dialogue among women. Feminism raises such problematic questions as (1) is feminism universal? or (2) is feminism a North American concept used by North American women to judge their sisters from other parts of the world? Certainly, if social issues are essential in the dialogue, little mutuality of understanding can occur between women who insist on interpreting the social conditions of their sisters from their own particular perspective.

Feminism is very complex, as are the feelings that it evokes in people. It can produce anger in those who feel oppressed, confusion in those who don't feel oppressed, and animosity in those accused of being the oppressors.

Adding to the complexity is another issue. If it is true that both religion and culture must be viewed together and that we cannot extract any religion from its cultural expression, the question of the universality of feminism must be addressed in a cultural-religious context. Does feminism mean the same to the Indian Christian as it does to the North American Christian, to the Theravadin Buddhist in Sri Lanka as to the Zen Buddhist in Japan, to the Iranian Shi'ite Muslim as to the Pakistani Sunni Muslim?

FEMINISM AS A WESTERN IDEA

Let us first examine the negative answer to the question of universal feminism. Many feminists and non-feminists alike criticize the women's movement because it sees the oppression of women as *the* paramount issue, not only in the United States but in the world. Leaders of the movement are accused of imposing their values and images of equality on other, very different cultures. Women who understand that they are oppressed and judge women of other cultures to be in the same situation, are often accused of imposing a Western interpretation of sexual equality on all women. Accordingly, the Western feminists, like the Western colonizers, have been called imperialistic. If a Western woman is going to engage in intercultural and interreligious dialogue, she needs at times to set aside her cultural perspective.

This is the lesson learned and recounted by one member of the Center for Women and Religion in Berkeley, California. After spending time in Buenos Aires, Argentina, she wrote:

> Typically, our [North American feminist] approach has been to share what we have, give from the largess of our experience, tell the world what has happened to us as women and what it means for them so that they, too, can be feminists. This, for all its good intentions, constitutes imperialism. Rather, I propose that in order to transform, to convert our imperialistic sharing into empowerment, we adopt a position of creative listening.[13]

Women must listen, not with the preconceived interpretation of what they will hear, but creatively, with the ability to be open to unexpected and unfamiliar experiences. When this listening is not done, when women believe that their view of women's rights is universal, much damage can occur in intercultural situations. North American women who have experienced the Third World have discovered that working or holding dialogue with women from these cultures requires the recognition of value systems that may differ radically from their own. They have come to appreciate the tension between individual rights and societal or family needs. Sometimes freeing women from the bondage of their families and advocating the dangerous state of unattached women is considered worse than enduring the prevailing patriarchy. Dedicated American feminists have been criticized by local women leaders for trying to design programs that assume greater individual autonomy than exists. Some efforts have been called counterproductive. It is obvious to the North American observer that the concept of individualism is not easily exportable.[14]

That Western feminists are often imperialistic was the view expressed by the Islamic feminist Riffat Hassan at a recent interreligious dialogue. Professor Hassan participated in a conference of women from five world traditions held at the Claremont Graduate School in California in April 1988. She warned North American women against assuming that they can speak for Islamic women, declaring, "I get very tired of Western women who tell me they sympathize with Islamic women without even knowing what Islamic feminists want."[15] Most Islamic women, according to Hassan, hope to combine marriage and a family with a job and a chance to participate in the policy-making process. "But Western feminists keep telling them that what they *should* want is autonomy in a non-patriarchal society and freedom from child bearing."[16]

Marjorie Suchocki, in an essay on interreligious dialogue, also issues a warning against absolutizing the idea of a liberated woman. She writes, "Interreligious dialogue at the societal/personal levels of justice will discover that what constitutes dignity will be defined differently in various cultures. There may be no single standard."[17] Moreover, it is not only impossible to absolutize woman's dignity, but it is even impossible to do so with the very concept of woman itself. Research by feminists shows the tremendous diversity of the meaning of womanhood. Varying cultural interpretations alert feminists that they cannot make any assumptions about woman as a category.[18]

To compound the problem further, phenomenological studies of various cultures indicate that what appear to Western eyes to be oppressive practices toward women may not be interpreted as such by the women themselves from within a culture. Such studies reveal that the stereotype of women as universally submissive and oppressed has no basis in fact. In one extensive study of women in north and central India, anthropologist Doranne Jacobson found that customs of veiling and seclusion of women can have positive connotations. In fact, to some women, purdah (the confinement of women to the home) is a mark of status. Poor Muslim women strive to remain housebound as much as possible, in emulation of the strict seclusion only wealthier Muslims can afford. Hindu women also consider themselves well-cared-for if their husbands can afford farmhands who free wives from the need to leave the courtyard.[19]

Contrary to what an American woman may think of such practices,

Jacobson does not believe that men consciously organize such systems to dominate women. She warns that it is really a mistake to see women as being restricted by men. Rather, both men and women play their part in a complex social and ecological system that runs reasonably smoothly, providing benefits to both sexes.[20]

This interpretation highlights the fact that North American women cannot base their judgment of women's status in other cultures on North American standards and values, at least not without an understanding of how the women who are native to other cultures interpret them.

The veiling and seclusion of women is also the topic of a study of Egyptian women done by Valerie J. Hoffman-Ladd. In an article in the *International Journal of Middle East Studies,* she examines (1) the writings of Muslim men and women, (2) their interpretations of the Qur'an, and (3) the daily lived experience of women in Egypt. In Egypt, women's liberation in Western style is to be avoided for political reasons; it speaks of Western imperialism and is therefore anti-Muslim. Women are urged to adopt Islamic values for the salvation of the nation, and are warned against imperialist plots to destroy Islamic society by "liberating" women in Western fashion.[21]

The situation in Iran is similar in that many women see veiling not as an oppressive practice but as one that firmly states their opposition to the West. Veiling has acquired a new symbolic meaning because of nationalism. The Islamic scarf, worn during the Revolution as protest against the Shah, is now also a sign of women's self-assertion against imported Westernism.[22]

Not only would the adoption of women's liberation be considered political acquiescence to Western imperialism, but it could also cause the type of collapse of sexual moral standards that has happened in the West. Adherence to modest dress standards and traditional norms can guard against such moral decline.[23] Many Islamic women do indeed equate the lifting of the veil with the exploitation of the female body by the male-dominated culture. An analogy might be made here between an Egyptian woman wearing a veil and a North American woman refusing to wear makeup or clothes that are considered sexually alluring. If we follow this analogy to its conclusion, we might better understand, then, that "wearing Islamic dress may in fact be a feminist stance in a society that is quick to make life for the unveiled woman insufferable."[24] Thus, when the cultural context is changed, what appears to be oppressive to a North American woman is actually liberating for an Egyptian woman.

In fact, Hoffman-Ladd concludes that the modesty and segregation of women are indeed positive practices. She states that "In this context, it is relatively easy to be persuaded that Islam offers woman a greater degree of dignity and self-esteem than Western Culture offers."[25] This is quite a different perspective from that which the average Western woman might have when she sees a veiled woman on a subway or on a television news broadcast. How dangerous it would be to bring our provincial understanding into an interreligious dialogue with Islamic women!

Polygamy is another practice that Western women have denounced as oppressive. However, upon reading a rationale for this practice in Ghana, we get a different perspective. Alice Appea, a National Organizer and Director of SOS Children's Village, tells us that polygamy was actually instigated by women. Because the wife felt unable to reap all the fields a man had cultivated, she permitted her husband to have another wife to help her. Although technology, Christianity, and education have served to change the attitudes toward polygamy, Appea tells us that "there are still some women who despite their education, would rather be the second or third than the only wife; they do not regard sex as exploitation of the female by the male."[26]

In women's dialogue, therefore, we need to question the concrete situation in which women live, and we need to understand the relativity of our own. Once we appreciate the variations in cultures, we realize that it is not entirely appropriate to apply the North American concept of autonomous liberation to the conditions and struggles of. women in other parts of the world. They have a different history and, consequently, a different story.

In conclusion, the Western idea of feminism is indeed imperialistic. The foregoing examples tell us that the standards of the women's movement are not uniform throughout the world and that Western feminists should not assume that they are. To the extent that this is true, we have a major problem in interreligious dialogue. We noted above that the conference held at Harvard in 1983 was centered on the topic of religion and social change. This very topic assumes that the participants shared a common concern for change. The women participating did hold the common viewpoint that they do suffer oppression and are working for its elimination. But did these women represent a sufficient segment of the population of their various cultures, or were they the select few who were Westernized enough to share the values of women from Europe and North America? We cannot really answer this question, but we need to ask it.

FEMINISM AS A UNIVERSAL IDEA

In contrast to the theories we have just explored, there is ample evidence both in academic and in popular literature to support the claim that there is a universal women's movement. Charlotte Bunch has conducted a study on the subject entitled *Passionate Politics: Feminist Theory in Action*, in which she observes that feminism exists throughout the world among women of every culture, color, and class. Regional problems are being addressed by indigenous movements of women which have expanded the meaning of feminism and the range of its tasks.[27]

To comprehend Bunch's conclusion that feminism is universal in spite of the many cultural differences among women, we need to reexamine and expand the definition of feminism. Can one envision a feminism that is not necessarily tied to the Western value system? One group of women had such a vision. Bunch describes the proceedings of a workshop on feminist ideology sponsored by the Asian and Pacific Centre for Women and Development in Bangkok in 1979 at which "women from each region presented what they were doing in relation to the themes of the UN Decade for Women."[28]

Understanding that the meaning of feminism is a major issue in any intercultural context, Bunch decries the media's sensationalist reports of the movement and attempts to present a more balanced view. She writes as follows:

> By acknowledging the power of the media's distortion of feminism at the Bangkok workshop, we were able to see the importance of defining it clearly for ourselves. Our definition brought together the right of every woman to equity, dignity, and freedom of choice through the power to control her own life and the removal of all forms of inequalities and oppression in society. We saw feminism as a world view that has an impact on all aspects of life, and affirmed the broad context of the assertion that the "personal is political." This is to say that the individual aspects of oppression and change are not separate from the need for political and institutional change.[29]

Bunch here responds to the common argument, found among political activists, that feminism is a selfish luxury of privileged women who are not concerned about issues of hunger, housing, or nuclear destruction. These attitudes falsely define feminism as a marginal movement concerned with "women's issues" rather than a broad political perspective on life.[30] In her analysis, Bunch examines the interconnectedness of social issues and women's issues and demonstrates how feminists are creating new interpretations and approaches to human rights, to development, to community and family, to conflict resolution, and so on.[31] When feminism is viewed in this broader political perspective, it can be seen as emerging everywhere. Women all over the globe are demonstrating a growing determination to be actors who participate in shaping society rather than remaining victims. There *is* such a thing as global feminism. Although there is much diversity and no central organization, there is a similarity in approaches and a fundamental questioning of society. Bunch believes that "while the particular forms that women's oppression takes in different settings vary and often pit some women against others, there is a commonality in the dynamic of domination by which women are subordinated to the demands, definitions, and desires of men."[32]

That this oppression is universal and connected to other injustices was also the observation of women attending the Nairobi conference. An American writing of her experiences in Kenya explains that

The domination of women isn't particular to any one country culture or religious group—it is a global reality. In a discussion on "Peace and Patriarchy," one woman succinctly stated, "How men treat women is central to solving global problems. If we can't learn to stop rape in the streets, we can't have peace." And if we don't work for justice, neither will we create peace on earth.[33]

Women who are not American also hold this view of an oppression that transcends cultural boundaries. In the opinion of one Iranian woman, Azar Tabari,

> Cultural Relativism becomes a banner under which oppression becomes tolerable. ... Fearful of the imaginary ghost of "cultural imperialism," many Western feminists silently watched the consolidation of a religious monstrosity. But why should geographical and cultural borders make what is conceived as oppression in one context an acceptable cultural norm in another?[34]

These words seem to conflict with the words that we heard from Riffat Hassan at the Claremont Conference. However, looking more closely at Tabari's arguments, we see that perhaps there might be some common ground. Tabari continues to say that "the element of choice . . . is crucial"[35] and that one must take that factor into consideration when looking at the traditional segregation of women. Yet this also was Riffat Hassan's point. The American cannot tell the Islamic woman what she should want. The Islamic woman must be free to choose. Tabari and Hassan seem to be in agreement, for both are saying that any imposition of values or behavior—whether it come from the male-dominated Islamic state or the North American feminist—is to be rejected. The Islamic woman must be free to choose for herself.

One indication that the consciousness of patriarchal oppression is worldwide is the growing number of women's groups mobilizing their strength to work for change. It is surprising to note that such groups are springing up in Third World countries as well.

One global organization is the Women's International Democratic Federation. Its journal of 1987 reported on the World Congress of Women that took place in Moscow from June 23 to June 27, 1987. This meeting gathered 2,823 women from 154 countries, representing 1,005 national organizations,[36] and was part of the series of events associated with the United Nations Decade for Women. The delegates expressed the desires of women from all social strata for a world without nuclear weapons, in which everybody strives to live and work in peace. They long for a world in which women can be secure and happy and can insure the same for the coming generations.

By joining forces, women are both learning from and giving support to each other as well as uniting their strength so that their voices and actions can make an impact. The Congress gave the women in Moscow "a feeling of confidence and strength . . . and stimulated their solidarity."[37]

We realize that this type of networking is going on all over the world when we read a few issues of a monthly pamphlet called *Women in Action*. The purpose of this magazine is to announce and report on conferences and organizations concerned with women's issues throughout the world. After reading page after page of these announcements, we develop a startling awareness of the presence of women who are working towards social change. Following is a sampling of events listed chronologically from just four issues in 1986 and 1987:

> April 18 to 24, 1986—Women from eight countries gathered together in the small village of Aragon, France to share experiences and discuss future strategies for the international solidarity network *Women Living Under Muslim Laws*. This was the network's first organized meeting since it grew out of an informal meeting of Muslim women in Europe in 1984.[38]

> Early 1986—The Arab Women Solidarity Association was created in early 1986 to strengthen ties between Arab women involved in social, cultural and educational activities. The networks' goals and activities are broad. It aims to promote the "active participation of women in the political, social and intellectual life" of their countries; to fight for "social justice within the family and in society"; and to encourage the development of "the identity and authentic personality of Arab women."[39]

> February 1986—The Association of African Women for Research and Development (AAWORD), a regional network of feminist scholars and development professionals, has been "relaunched" to improve and expand its activities throughout Africa.[40]

> 1987—Feminist Forum represents approximately 200 women of 18 different nationalities, based in Japan. It publishes a newsletter, "Feminist Forum," and was established to promote feminist communication among women in Japan.[41]

> 1987—The Kadin Cevresi (Women's Circle) is an Istanbul-based publishing collective that aims to produce books, organize conferences and events and provide a communication network for women in Turkey.[42]

> 1987—The Centre for Women's Development was founded in Sri Lanka in 1983 to educate, organize and mobilize rural women to work

for their own emancipation. It was originally a local organization confined to villages but has now grown into a national organization with activities throughout the country.[43]

1987—Shakti was created to fill the need for good, scientific research designed to influence and develop policy on various issues of key concern to women and development [in India].[44]

1987—WINA [Women's Institute for New Awakening] focuses on education of women for new awareness and seeks to promote this awareness through education, research, oral histories, investigative studies and publications [in India].[45]

These organizations may vary in size and may not necessarily represent the female population of a given country, but their existence in increasingly large numbers indicates a consciousness that has germinated and is apparently growing across the globe. Western women working for change can no longer sit back and say that women in other countries are so different that they cannot be called their sisters.

Another publication that produces a similar effect is a collection of comments by women who gathered for a meeting of the Women's International League for Peace and Freedom in Geneva in 1987. Women contributors spoke of both the accomplishments and needs of women in their respective countries. Jae Hee Kim, the representative from Korea, reported that "Though sexual equality is far from complete in Korea, steps have been taken. . . . Women's groups and others are working to alter public opinion towards understanding the desire of all women to develop themselves."[46]

A judge from Accra, Ghana, Annie Jiagge, spoke of the need for women throughout the world to accept that form of feminism which connects women's issues and global concerns. In her opinion,

The liberation of women all over the world, across all barriers and frontiers, bound in mutual support, must mark the beginning of the end of national patriotism . . . and herald the dawn of world patriotism which knows no geographical, racial or ideological boundaries.
A truly liberated woman's vision is clear for all injustice.[47]

It would appear from our sampling of meetings, organizations, and conferences that feminism, as defined in its broader and more inclusive context of economic, political, and personal equality for all peoples, is indeed a global concept.

There are also several publications that, rather than report happenings, collect historical data and essays from scholars in countries throughout the world. One such collection is an anthology of women's history edited by

Robin Morgan, entitled *Sisterhood is Global*. A sampling of collections includes essays about Egypt, India, and Israel. After recounting the rise and decline of the women's movement in Egypt in this century, Nawaal El Saadawi writes that "women have begun the long, hard road to liberation, and everywhere ... we will continue."[48] Devaki Jain recounts stories of women's activity that produced economic and political liberation in India. From them she concludes, "The ability of women to identify their common problem and perceive a solution that requires steel-like courage and great risk to life but still is a *nonviolent* method is well illustrated."[49] From Israel, Shulamit Aloni tells us that "Women ... have started becoming aware of their rights (or lack of them). The whole world has become smaller and more open. We know what is happening everywhere."[50]

In addition to reports of organizations and conferences, and to collections of data and essays, there exists an international women's quarterly called *Connexions*, published in California, which is the "collective product of feminists of diverse nationalities and political perspectives committed to contributing to an international women's movement."[51] The editors of this publication understand that

> Women do not live in a vacuum, but in what is still largely a man's world. It is essential for us to understand the working of that world if we are to understand each other. We hope that *Connexions* will be one step toward building an international women's movement.[52]

The 1988 issue is dedicated to the stories of girls and concerned women in seventeen countries who demonstrate "tenacity, resourcefulness and courage in transcending the inveterately low and restrictive expectations their cultures attempt to impose on them."[53]

In conclusion, let it be noted that the beginning of this chapter recorded opinions that consider feminism to be a Western idea that does not apply to other parts of the world. This attitude is opposed to that just mentioned, that is, the universality of feminism. The fact that these two opposing views are prominent in the discussions of women indicates the seriousness of this problem. Thus far, the issue has not been considered in interreligious dialogue.

The problems that have been touched upon in the above data appear to be twofold. First, the definition of feminism has both a narrow and a broad definition. The literalist might say that it is a movement that advocates woman's liberation through autonomy. A broader definition might include the struggle for justice and liberation in all those areas of life that encompass women's concerns. Such areas include feeding children, building a nuclear-free world for them, protecting their environment, and eliminating racism. I would suggest that the broader definition is the more accurate because of its universal applicability and its wholistic vision that connects the world's problems. No one issue is the exclusive worry of any particular people.

The second issue raised regarding the universality of feminism is the difference between the fact of oppression and the awareness of oppression. From the above information, it would appear that there is a feminist movement that has grown out of women's oppressed situations and that is working to eliminate such situations in all parts of the globe. However, it has not yet engaged the majority of women who remain acculturated in male-dominated systems and who accept these patterns as the given social order. For example, those women in Africa who consider polygamy good (because there are more women to share the work) do not understand that the work load itself is a burden to women. Labeling situations as oppressive is a delicate matter that demands serious consultation and consideration. Furthermore, educating towards the awareness of oppression is even more problematic in that making judgments and exercising power—as in the teacher-student situation—can produce very sensitive issues in the context of dialogue. While I do not propose that the dialogue table serve as the classroom for such education, it can and most likely will be the raw material out of which a new self-awareness will begin to be woven.

7

Is Religion Liberating?

TENSION IN WOMEN'S ATTITUDES

The issues presented by the inherent connection of the religious with the socio-political realms must now come to terms with conflicting attitudes toward religion as a liberating force. Participants in interreligious dialogue have until recently been assumed to be practitioners within their individual traditions and were therefore engaged in apologetics for their own particular religions. However, the issues of women's oppression and feminism have introduced the problem of the critique of religions from those *within* its borders. Women, in past dialogues, often came together with a common interest in liberation and in critiquing the androcentrism of their religions. This common bond was taken as a plus for women's dialogue that united them in ways not open to men. An example of this attitude was expressed in the published version of the major papers given at two dialogues among Jewish, Christian, and Islamic women, one in November 1980 and a second in January 1984. Jeanne Audrey Powers writes in the introductory essay:

> because each participant knows what it means for women to be silenced or rendered insignificant in her own tradition, a special kind of hearing and openness in listening takes place. Sensitivity toward differing positions is crucial in dialogue, and the common experiences of women that run through all of the traditions make dialogue uniquely possible for women.[1]

This perspective may be true for these specific dialogues, but I disagree with those who would apply this principle to all interreligious dialogues among women. The idea of a common experience of women that runs through all traditions is greatly simplified; gatherings in which this is the case are composed of very select individuals. If, however, we are interested in getting a more realistic picture of women in the world's religions, we would not find such unity.

My skepticism is born out of an experience at an interreligious dialogue, mentioned above, which took place in Claremont, California in the spring of 1988. Nine women representing five major traditions gathered with a group of approximately fifty spectators who also contributed to the discussions. These women were chosen not for any common attitudes that they held but simply because they were prominent practitioners and scholars of their particular religions. What emerged was an amazing diversity of attitudes towards religion in general and towards particular religions individually. The diverse views showed not an advantage to women's dialogue but rather a unique disadvantage. The specific problem lies in the fact that while some women did view their religious tradition as oppressive, others saw it as very liberating. This tension in women's attitudes can be quickly seen in a review of women's writings from within the traditions of Christianity, Judaism, Islam, and Buddhism. Understanding that this is not a complete list of world religions, we present it to illustrate a point rather than as a thorough explanation.

CHRISTIANITY

We deal with Christianity first because it is the religion that the popular white Western feminist movement began considering first, and the one that those practicing theology in the Americas have had most contact with. Within Christianity we find the gamut of reactions by women, from complete acceptance to critical partial acceptance to complete rejection. Those who have rejected the tradition have begun what they consider a new phase of religious awareness and consider themselves post-Christian.

An example of the diversity of attitudes toward Christianity is illustrated by a survey taken by the Catholic Bishops of America in 1988 in preparation for their letter regarding women's concerns. While the letter itself can be interpreted variously, it is interesting to read comments by specific women. Although many express concern over the Catholic teaching on divorce and contraception, others have very positive things to say. For example, one woman from St. Petersburg, Florida, notes as follows:

> The Catholic community is "my people." I could never be at home anywhere else ... The Catholic Church has greatly shaped my identity and provided me with fundamental values and a spirituality that I will always live by. It has done the same for my family as well.[2]

Other comments include:

> Mothering is surely the most difficult role I've been assigned to fulfill and I'm glad the church recognizes what a contribution it is.[3]

Most women welcome ... developments in the church ... They also honor in faith the church's doctrine and values, its moral standards and life of prayer, its liturgy, and especially the eucharist, which "is still the most compelling force in the church today."[4]

Monika Hellwig, a prominent Catholic theologian, urges women to approach the task of confronting the institution while maintaining the value of its traditions. She writes in *Commonweal*, "Our immediate challenge is to move beyond submissive passivity in the affairs of society without indulging in angry rejection of the traditions of our faith or in aggressively competitive self-promotion . . ."[5] Some of the more radical suggestions coming from Christian women regarding their attempt to achieve decision-making positions in the Church might be interpreted by Hellwig as self-promotion. This view can be considered a conservative one and might meet considerable opposition at a dialogue with women who see an urgent need to take more drastic measures towards liberation.

Another conservative perspective is presented by the Orthodox Christian theologian, Deborah Belonick. In an article on revelation and metaphors, she responds to the Christian feminist critique of the male terms used for God. While some feminists consider the language to be oppressive and exclusive of women's experience, Belonick wants to maintain the male image as essential for Orthodox theology of the Trinity. In this way she holds the view that her Church and its expressions for the Godhead are liberating in their accuracy. She cites the argument of Gregory of Nyssa who calls God "Father" because it best expresses his relationship with the Son as a second person, co-equal and co-eternal with God. According to Belonick, fathering and mothering are two distinct functions. Fathering is associated with initiating a generation or begetting life, whereas mothering connotes conceiving life or bringing it to fruition. Since God's action in the Trinity is one of generating and begetting, it is *fatherhood* and not *motherhood* that accurately describes His mode of life.[6]

One can easily imagine the reaction of some other Christian feminist theologians who have made a strong case against the use of the term "father," as has Rosemary Ruether in *Sexism and God-Talk* and Sallie McFague in *Metaphorical Theology*. The theological arguments both for and against the traditional use of the term "father" for God are grounded in the Christian tradition. These differences represent a variety of feminist attitudes within Christianity.

Yet another viewpoint is presented by black Christian women. In a lecture on womanist theology given at the School of Theology at Claremont, California, Delores Williams spoke of the black woman's view of Christ and Christianity. She insists that while the black womanist movement has its roots in feminism, it differs in many respects. The black woman seeks liberation not only for herself but for her family, and her efforts therefore are directed not so much in opposing patriarchy as toward the broader social systems of society. Her theology is biblically based and she has no problem with the maleness of Christ. She eloquently states that "a system nailed him to a true cross and the miracle raised him from the dead . . . The Resurrection story has become integrated into the people"[7] as a sign of liberation in both this world and the next. Therefore, the concept of Goddess is "not terribly important for [black women]."[8] For Williams, the resurrected savior of biblical Christianity has liberated her people; that this savior is male and not female is of no significance and does not affect the spirituality of black women.

Biblical Christianity is liberating also for the Asian woman. One Asian Christian, Kwok Pui Lan, warns those feminists who are moving away from the biblical tradition that "they tend to alienate themselves from global sisterhood because the Bible is an important part of our common 'heritage' and 'language.' "[9] She understands that Elizabeth Schüssler Fiorenza's hermeneutics, which puts the struggle for liberation in a social context, can be used by Asian women to interpret the Bible as a source of women's liberation, rather than as a proof text for oppression. Thus, the Asian woman, like the black woman, clings to the biblical text and its imagery as her hope and her freedom.

A slightly more radical stance against the patriarchy in Christianity is taken by Rosemary Radford Ruether. Her work does keep her within the walls of the Christian tradition because she maintains its basic doctrines and tenets, but at the same time, she reinterprets them. In so doing, she assigns them a more egalitarian meaning so as to purge Christianity of its sin of patriarchy. She develops an inclusive Christology, ecclesiology, and sacramentology that are systematically represented in her study *Sexism and God-Talk.*

Ruether maintains the belief in the divinity of Christ but prefers to strip it of its traditional masculine imagery by not encapsulating it " 'once-for-all' in the historical Jesus."[10] Rather, she advocates that the continuence of Christ's identity be understood in the Christian community. Once this is done, she writes, "the Jesus of the synoptic Gospels can be recognized as a figure remarkably compatible with feminism."[11]

The importance of sacramental life is also emphasized by Ruether. Her critical concern is not the sacraments but the clericalism in which they are embedded. "The liberation of the Church from clericalism also means reclaiming the sacraments as expressions of the redemptive life of the Church that the people are empowered to administer collectively."[12] She advocates that the members of the community become skilled and empowered to minister, and she offers ways in which this can happen. Neither the Catholic nor Protestant Eucharist "must be exercised by persons set aside in specialized ministry."[13] The sacraments should rather be performed and interpreted by the community in such a way as to reflect its collective experience of grace.

Ruether's position within the Church is in opposition to other feminists who see both the ideology and the practices of the institution so steeped in patriarchy that it is beyond redemption. Mary Daly is among those women now labeled as post-Christian who express their faith in other forms such as the Goddess religion or the Wicca movement. In an essay published in 1979, Daly wrote that "we are being called upon to recognize the poverty of all symbols and the fact of our past idolatry regarding them and to turn to our own resources for bringing about the radically new in our own lives."[14] The resources of Daly and those like her have been rich and plentiful since then and serve to remind us that the critique of Christianity has become increasingly radical. Any interreligious dialogue of women, to be truly inclusive, would necessarily have to include the views of these women.

Even if a dialogue does not represent the entire range of attitudes towards Christianity, those in dialogue must recognize the existence of these attitudes. Because of these points of view, it can never be assumed that Christian women engaging in dialogue have a common perspective out of which they speak. It is possible that there may be more disagreement and less commonality among Christians than between Christians and adherents of other religions.

JUDAISM

Women in Judaism are experiencing the same type of diversity among themselves as are the Christian women. Some hold that their feminist concerns are compatible with traditional Judaism; others believe that Judaism must enter into a new era in order to be egalitarian. In an article explaining the gamut of thinking in this area, Susannah Heschel writes, "At issue in all the approaches are both the relationships of women to Jewish history and tradition and feminism as a mode of reinterpreting Judaism."[15]

At the traditional end of the spectrum is Blu Greenberg, who explains her position at length in a now famous book, *On Women and Judaism: A View from Tradition*. She is interested in preserving most of the Jewish tradition and conveys a very positive and hopeful attitude towards it. In her opinion, "What often is overlooked today is that, over the ages, Jewish tradition by and large, has upgraded the status of women."[16] Because Greenberg understands that the Halakhah (Jewish law) had responded to changes in society at large,[17] she can argue that "Necessary changes can be wrought in keeping with the tenets and spirit of Halakhah."[18]

For Greenberg, feminist concerns are therefore very much compatible with the basic laws of Judaism and can be incorporated without a rejection of any of the values of the tradition. Her book explains how she interprets Orthodox Jewish practices, some of which are seen as clearly oppressive to more liberal feminist Jews. For example, she devotes much space to explaining why she still observes the practices of niddah and mikveh (abstaining from sexual relations during menstruation and for seven days after, until the mikveh or ritual cleansing is performed). An example of Greenberg's reasoning is seen in her explanation of the advantage of such practices:

> As I go about my business at the mikveh, I often savor the knowledge that I am doing exactly as Jewish women have done for twenty or thirty centuries. It is a matter not only of keeping the chain going, but also one of self-definition: this is how my forebearers defined themselves as Jewish women and as part of the community and this is how I define myself. It is this sense of community with them that pleases me.[19]

But besides putting her in touch with the broader community and establishing her identity as a Jewish woman, these Orthodox practices enable her interpersonal relationship to grow and develop in ways "appropriate to its ebb and flow."[20]

While Greenberg may sometimes find conflict between Jewish tradition and feminist equality,[21] she represents those Jewish women who have a basically positive attitude toward their religion, not merely because they follow it unquestioningly, but because they have come to appreciate its richness and integrity. She writes:

> my critique [of Halakhah] could grow only out of a profound appreciation for the system in its entirety; its ability to preserve the essence of an ancient revelation as a fresh experience each day; its power to generate an abiding sense of kinship, past and present, its intimate relatedness to concerns both immediate and other-worldly; its psychological soundness; its ethical and moral integrity. On the whole I believe that a Jew has a better chance of living a worthwhile life if he or she lives a life according to Halakhah . . .[22]

According to the *Los Angeles Times* of February 7, 1989, Greenberg is not alone. This very positive attitude toward Orthodox Judaism is shared by other modern professional women, three of whom are represented in an article entitled "Modern Women Explain Return to Orthodoxy." An artist, Judith Margolis, corroborates Greenberg's attitude about mikveh. She claims that the laws regarding abstinence and the ritual bath have helped her marriage by putting some limits on intimate contact. "Orthodox practice," she says, "allows a person to have time alone. I experience myself. And that turns out to be supportive of [my] creative work."[23] Observance of the Sabbath also holds out a very practical advantage for Margolis: "By keeping the Sabbath, I take one day when I cannot be striving . . . It's a day when I have to rest. It energizes me enormously."[24]

Sharon Schwartz Brooks, a Harvard-trained physician who is also practicing Orthodoxy, agrees with Greenberg that it is important to have a connection with a people and its history. This connection in turn gives her a sense of the divine, and her religion has become a "vital, mystical part of her world."[25] These women who have embraced Orthodoxy are newsworthy because the strict laws of Judaism appear to be antithetical to the life-style of a modern woman. Obviously to some modern women, there is no antithesis but rather a compatibility and even, for them, a necessary correlation.

A larger portion of the work being done by Jewish feminists today, however, takes a more radical approach to the traditions, and is critical of Greenberg's work. Susannah Heschel, for example, claims that Greenberg's approach does not represent a coherent theological position and employs the historical method in some areas but not in others.[26] Heschel's view of the traditions of Judaism is not as positive as that of Greenberg. In fact, according to Heschel, Judaism, in the way it has existed for nearly two thousand years, has died. Feminist concerns and the responses they have evoked reveal the absence of a coherent position regarding the authority of Jewish law in an age of relativism. They also reveal general confusion over what constitutes Judaism in today's context of pluralism and free choice.[27] Heschel sees that the main core of diversity among Jewish women lies in "whether feminists are explicating the deeper meaning of Jewish tradition or grafting onto it their own, new concerns."[28]

One Jewish feminist who is attempting to explore these deeper meanings of Judaism is Drorah Setel. She uses feminist theory to examine key concepts, not only to understand them better but also to find a more inclusive interpretation. Modern feminist theory has critiqued separatist thought that divides reality into opposing dualisms and has responded by placing value on relationality. Setel applies this feminist viewpoint to the Hebrew concept of holiness. What role does relationship play in the Jewish tradition? Furthermore, what role can it play when so much of Judaism incorporates patriarchal modes of thought in the form of dualistic separations? The question is particularly significant because *kadosh,* the Hebrew word commonly translated into English as "holy" in fact means "separate" or "set apart."[29] This idea of separateness, according to Setel, implies an oppositional dualism between and among peoples that is a patriarchal mode of thought. Therefore, Setel asks if there is a more relational way the concept of holiness can be expressed in Judaic thought. She discovers that "the tradition itself contains significant alternatives to separation as the model of holiness,"[30] and, if emphasized, they would produce a shift in the traditional conception of Judaism. To shift is not to leave the tradition behind but rather to turn one's attention in a different direction, one which might not be within the vision of a more traditional Jewish woman such as Blu Greenberg.

Monotheism is another issue of concern to Setel. She calls it a "vulgar monotheism"[31] because it is concerned, not with a belief in one God/dess but rather with the "belief in one *image* of God/dess."[32] According to Setel, we can examine various images of the divine without endangering the essence of Jewish faith. These reinterpretations represent one aspect of Jewish feminism that may not be agreed upon by others who are considering women's place within the religion.

Issues of diversity, however, emerge even in a group of more liberal Jewish feminists. An example of such diversity is found in one group consisting of rabbis, professors, therapists, social service workers, theologians, and others who meet yearly for support and spiritual enrichment. All, committed to Judaism within the context of the Conservative or Reform movements,[33] met originally with the assumption that they held common concerns but realized, soon after coming together, that their differences were greater than they had expected. One member, Martha A. Ackelsberg, recounts that dealing with such diversity was not only a difficult experience but a very powerful one as well. The women's individual differences came out most strongly in their experience of *davvening* (communal prayer), because, as Ackelsberg writes,

> Though we knew we wanted to pray in a feminist way, to a feminist God, we realized that we imaged the God we did (or could) pray to in very different ways. . . . What would it mean, for example, to image God as feminine? Some wished to explore the usefulness of Goddess imagery; others reacted strongly against doing so, citing the Jewish tradition's identification of Goddess-worship with idolatry, and the notion of Goddess as antithetical to the God of Israel.[34]

When we read of these differing opinions, it would seem as though the women are from several religious traditions rather than from one Judaism. And herein lies the issue. When it comes to a feminist critique, the difference in attitudes even among those who are nominally feminists within one religion are as great as those found between women of different religious traditions. Moreover, the greater the assumed similarities among the women, the greater the frustration caused by the differences.

Of her particular group, Ackelsberg writes,

> Given our common commitment to transforming Jewish tradition and practice, and the hopes and expectations we had in doing so together, it is not surprising that our efforts at creativity generate high levels of frustration and anger. . . . The resolution we seem to have achieved has elements of what I take to be the "feminist ideal": namely a community not only accepting of, but thriving on, diversity.[35]

Thus we understand that Jewish women have different views of the extent to which Jewish law and tradition have been oppressive towards them. Thus Jewish women, like their Christian sisters, defy categorization — a crucial fact to understand in dialogue.

ISLAM

In a previous chapter, when exploring the universality of feminism, we noted that some women subjected to segregation and veiling did not consider their situation as oppressive. The reasons given were based on the cultural and national environment in which the practices took place. Here, however, the concentration is on the religious context of these practices, most of which are found in Islamic countries. While many Westerners do not expect to find feminist movements within Islam, the truth is that they do exist and these movements are at least as varied as those within Christianity and Judaism. The fact is that most Westerners view Islam as a misogynistic religion, without understanding or examining the real position of women taught by Islam. One Jordanian writer notes that "a lot of writing about women in the Arab world or (especially) women in the Muslim world starts from the premise that Islam is a conservative religion, that it's holding women back."[36] Even some of the women who are fighting for change within the Muslim countries deny that change can come about through a renewed religious perspective. They seek social, economic, and educational change only. One Islamic woman, writing in a Pakistani journal, assumes that the Qur'an explicitly teaches the inferiority of women:

> difficulty arises when an attempt is made to reinterpret those Qur'anic injunctions which clearly establish male superiority over women . . . it seems clear that if women's movements aim at achieving the afore-mentioned objective under the Islamic system, they are trying in vain, as Islam, being a patriarchal system, can never grant such concessions which may weaken the bases of its social structure.[37]

However, when we read the writings of women who are studying as well as practicing the religion of Islam, we find that their view of the Qur'an is very different. They tell us that it is possible to work for the equality and liberation of women while having a strong faith in Islam and being a loyal follower of Muhammad. Most of the women writing from within Islam view Muhammad and the Qur'an as very egalitarian; their disagreement lies in the degree to which the *Hadith* (tradition) and the *Sharia* (Muslim law) have imposed an oppressive system.

On the most conservative end of the spectrum, we find some Islamic women maintaining their equality with men, but they understand this equality in a way that differs from the Western version. Because of their innate biological and psychological differences, the roles of men and women are clearly defined. These roles, while different, are nevertheless equal in importance and value. According to the American Islamic scholar, Jane I. Smith, there exists the understanding that women can best be fulfilled in marriage and through the bearing of children. Also, within the marriage, it is necessary for one partner to have final authority. This hierarchy is divinely ordained and therefore is a *natural* circumstance.[38]

Many Muslim women also believe that their role in society as well as in the family is divinely ordained. Women, because they bear children, are innately nurturers and homemakers, while men work in the public forum and are responsible for the financial support and physical protection of the family.

This attitude is illustrated by some of the recorded comments of Islamic women in India cited in a study done by Jamila Brijbhushan. She quotes several women who are in polygamous marriages:

"we lived together quite happily and three of us became close friends" ... asserts a social worker ...

"Yes," agreed a worker in a Cooperative Society, ... "as long as your husband treats you well there is no hardship to being a co-wife."

"I brought my best friend as my co-wife," said a middle-aged woman whose husband works as a clerk in a Government office, "because I could not have children."[39]

These women firmly believe that men and women have very different roles in family life. The author continues:

The arguments for polygamy stress the absolute necessity for a women to have a man's protection. "Where would she go otherwise?" asked a middle-aged widow. "Take the case of a widow I know," said a social worker ... With three grown up daughters what can she do? ... Marriage is the only protection there is or can be. Does she or her daughters care if they become only wives or co-wives? Their urgent need is to have a roof over their heads, enough to eat and the protection of a man ...[40]

In contrast to this view (which understands that the division of the sexes is natural and therefore divinely ordained) is the attitude that they are changeable because they are cultural. This belief is held by Fatima Mernissi in her study of women in Islam, *Beyond the Veil*. She understands that "the Muslim marriage is based on male dominance,"[41] but, this marriage is not ordained by Allah; rather it was "one of the devices the Prophet used to implement the *Umma* [and] was quite unlike any existing sexual unions."[42] In other words, the attitude is subject to change. Mernissi does not believe that Islam teaches women's inherent inferiority. In fact, she says it affirms the potential equality between the sexes. The existing inequality is blamed rather on the specific social institutions designed to restrain woman's power: namely, segregation and legal subordination of the woman to the man in the family structure.[43]

This discrepancy of views among Muslim women is clearly seen in Pakistan. In an essay in the anthology *Sisterhood is Global*, Miriam Habib notes different interpretations of the Qur'an. One given by Muslim modernists claims that Islam as a faith and a system has proven to be the greatest liberator of women. The conservative view, on the other hand, uses the scriptures to argue a subservient position for women.[44]

The situation in Pakistan is detailed further by Anita Weiss in an article in *Asian Survey*. She reports that in 1982 the president established a commission called the Ansari Commission to inform him of any occurrences that went against Islam. Under this commission women were disqualified from ever being heads of state, prohibited from leaving the country without a male escort, and unable to serve abroad in the foreign service.[45]

In reporting on the reaction to this commission,Weiss has described the type of discrepancies that cause problems in dialogue. She writes about women's groups such as Women's Action Forum and the All-Pakistan Women's Association, which have taken a strong stand against the Ansari Commission on the grounds that "some clauses about women . . . are repugnant to the Holy Qur'an and Islam, which gives women equal rights with men in all public matters."[46]

Nonetheless, Weiss adds that not all women reject the reactionary reforms and the work of the Commission. She reports that another women's group has actually "dismissed the validity of the U.N. Charter on the Elimination of Discrimination Against Women by calling it an anti-Islamic document."[47]

It is not only in Pakistan that such disagreements arise over Qur'anic interpretation and women. Adele Ferdows notes than even in Iran, where women seem to be returning to traditional patterns and practices, there are women reconsidering their place in Islam. She writes, "below the surface an intellectual movement seems to be brewing which is reflected in the few essays published which analyze women's rights on the basis of a reinterpretation of the Qur'an."[48] Throughout the Muslim world, the twentieth century has opened up not merely a secular movement but a religious revivalism that looks to the Qur'an rather than to its later interpretations for the precepts of life. According to Yvonne Yazbeck Haddad, a special genre of literature has arisen that extols the elevated and liberating role Islam has assigned to woman. Women's rights are guaranteed by Islam and include her right to be educated, to inherit, to keep her maiden name, to carry on her own business transactions, and to maintain her wealth.[49]

This liberating aspect of the Qur'an was a theme at a meeting of Muslim feminists that took place at Radcliffe College in 1984. The discussion was reported on in an issue of *Unitarian Universalist World*. The key lecture was given by Benazir Bhutto, then the Acting Chair, but now President of Pakistan. The authors report that "In interviews with Muslim women during and after the conference, we were surprised at the extent to which they presented a feminism based on the Quoran [sic]."[50] One of the speakers, Negiba Magademni, reports that in her studies she realized that the Qur'an was far more liberating than she had been brought up to believe. The practices that she now considered oppressive were not in the Qur'an but were added later in the *Hadith* and other commentaries. For example, "The Quoran does not call for veiling of women but simply enjoins both men and women to dress and act with decorum."[51] For this reason, Magademni urges Islamic feminists to "focus on the Quoran . . . rather than the commentaries that followed."[52]

When asked about those *suras* in the Qur'an that appeared to give men privileges denied to women, Magademni responds,

> This came about because of a language problem. . . . The Quoran was the first great work of literature in Arabic. However, each tribe had a different meaning for each word. Later, as conservative men began to interpret the Quoran they gave valuations and interpretations to various words that fit their own prejudices and political ambitions.[53]

Also considering the Qur'an as the liberator of woman is Riffat Hassan, a Qur'anic scholar from Pakistan who teaches in the United States. She has dedicated herself to working on a feminist exegesis and understands that the Qur'an alone, not the *Hadith* or *Shariah,* is the inspired book of Islam. As long as arguments are based on the Qur'an, claims Hassan, "they can't accuse you of importing Western-style feminism."[54]

Riffat Hassan's work on Qur'anic interpretation has been widely published, and an early article appeared in the *Journal of Ecumenical Studies*. In it she writes:

> Having spent seven years in the study of the Qur'anic passages relating to women, I am convinced that the Qur'an is not biased against women and does not discriminate against them. . . . But the interpretations of the Qur'an by men (women to this day have never had the right to interpret the Qur'an) have distorted the truth almost beyond recognition and have made the Qur'an a means of keeping women in bondage, physically and spiritually.[55]

A large portion of this article is dedicated to explaining the discrepancy between Qur'anic texts and the practices in Islamic countries. Hassan quotes the *suras* on marriage, divorce, and polygamy. A sampling of her arguments regards women's dress.

> Although the purpose of the Qur'anic legislation dealing with women's dress and conduct (Sura 24:30–31; 33:59) was to make it safe for women to go about their daily business (since they have the right to

earn money, as witnessed by Sura 4:32) without fear of sexual harass-
ment, Muslim societies have put many of them behind veils and locked
doors on the pretext of protecting their chastity, forgetting that
according to the Qur'an (Sura 4:15) confinement to their homes was
not the normal way of life for chaste women but a punishment for
"unchastity."[56]

In summary, we notice that writings about and by Muslim women indicate a variety of attitudes towards the Qur'an and its interpretation. While
all of the women referred to in this section are practicing Muslims who
believe that Islam is liberating, their varying interpretations of the Qur'an
indicate very different boundaries in which this liberation is found. The
conservative women understand that the *Hadith* and *Shariah* are sacred and
believe that the separation of sex roles is divinely ordained; hence they
believe women should behave accordingly. The more liberal women view
only the Qur'an as inspired and the other works of Islam as human, that
is, male, interpretations that are in need of change. These women see that
the Qur'an advances the equality of women in that its definition of sex roles
is minimal and flexible. Furthermore, among these liberal women who wish
to return to the roots of the Qur'an, there are various interpretations of
the different *suras*, such that the scholarly study becomes an arena itself
for the discussion of the place of women in Islam.

Unless these variations are understood, it will be difficult to hold dialogue with Muslim women. Although Muslim men may also have these
various views of Qur'anic interpretation, the differences will probably be
less pronounced in dialogue because men are not so personally and visibly
affected by such variations on interpretation in their everyday lives.

BUDDHISM

In Chapter 5 we cited Buddhism as a religion that stressed a non-per-
sonal ultimate reality. We noted that an egalitarian philosophy was compatible with this religion. However, when we examine the work of women
Buddhists and Buddhist scholars we discover that in practice Buddhism has
held various stances toward women. The complexity of the issues is compounded when one considers that Buddhism has developed several sects
and that each of these sects has taken on new forms as they have traveled
to different cultures.

It cannot be denied that much of Buddhist tradition has been misogynistic. Rita Gross, an American scholar who is both a feminist and a practicing Buddhist, has written extensively on the connection between the two
ideologies. In one article she admits that "It is difficult to avoid the conclusion that Buddhism has, classically, been more a men's religion than
human religion and that women's access to the fullness and depth of the
tradition has been somewhat less than exemplary."[57]

Another American scholar, Diana Paul, who has done a thorough study of women in Buddhist writings, concedes that misogyny is the dominant attitude in Buddhism. She notes that while discrimination (viewed as the imagination's tendency to posit innate qualities onto things) was condemned, latent discrimination based upon sex was continued. The theme of "sexual transformation" in Buddhist writings stereotyped the female as biologically and psychologically limited. Hence, removal of sex as obstacle to enlightenment meant being transformed from female to male.[58]

A Japanese scholar, Kumiko Uchino, who spoke at the 1983 Harvard conference on Women and Religion, agrees that Buddhism is a sexist religion. In discussing the status of Soto nuns in Japan, she recalls that "In the Buddhist tradition, women are regarded as impure, having a more sinful *karma* than men and unable to attain Buddhahood."[59] She then explains how, in the early part of this century, nuns worked in an equality movement to obtain educational opportunities. From Uchino's point of view, Buddhism itself is not very egalitarian, but women within it have been able to work for change.

Western versions of Buddhism have also treated women unequally: far fewer women than men have become accomplished Dharma practitioners and teachers. In fact, Rita Gross notes that "women have often had little access to practice at all."[60] She attributes this situation to the fact that "Buddhist institutions support and encourage the dharmic potential of men more effectively than they support and encourage women's potential for enlightenment."[61]

The situation is changing, however, and changing for good reason. Some feminists recognize that at the core of the Buddha's message there is an egalitarian ideal, and that ideal is beginning to be recognized and taught.

Speaking at the interreligious dialogue held in Claremont, Eiko Kawamura, a professor at Hanazono University in Kyoto, discussed the heart of Zen Buddhism. Her perception is that its teachings aim to transcend sexual differences or rather sexuality itself. The Buddha-nature that transcends all distinctions "is intrinsic to all beings."[62] In a working paper that was discussed in preparation for the conference, she wrote,

> If the feminist movement were to base itself upon the kind of elucidation of the self as is carried out in Zen, then a completely new dimension would unfold at the fundamental locus of openness, and the many directions of the feminist movement would take on a new vitality fueled by the integrity of truth.[63]

Here Zen Buddhism is viewed by a Japanese woman in a very positive way, as a vehicle of liberation from the perspective of its goal and meditative practice. According to Kawamura, the social issue or horizontal dimension of feminism would resolve itself if one were, through the practice of meditation, to seek one's identity "not only in ourselves but also in nature and in the absolutely opened openness,"[64] if one could transcend the bondage of the substance of sexuality.

Rita Gross also appreciates the liberating aspect of Buddhism, which she understands is in its basic teaching but not necessarily in its practice. Although she agrees that Buddhism is egalitarian, she differs with the view that to be liberating Buddhism must transcend sexuality. She, like other American Buddhist women, understands that the Buddhist ideal of enlightenment does not require the transcending of the bodily self but rather an engagement of that self. The physical world and the society are to be transformed and universal well-being is to be achieved through social action: herein lies the central goal of Mahayana Buddhism.

Other American Buddhist women also see Buddhism as a liberating philosophy, in its ideal and practice, as well as in its vertical and horizontal dimensions. One imagines that these women have used their experience of feminism to influence and interpret their perception of Buddhism. This impression is supported by Rita Gross in her description of the type of liberation experienced by the American Buddhist. It is, she says, a "wonder of the *coincidence* of the arrival of great Buddhist teachers in the West and emergence of the Western feminist movement."[65]

A recent compilation of talks by American Buddhist women, *A Gathering of Spirit*, has been edited by Ellen S. Sidor. She writes about a

new spiritual culture: women practicing and teaching Buddhism in America. Never before in the history of Buddhism, and probably not since the long-ago days at the height of Goddess worship, have women played so prominent a role in directing their own spiritual lives.[66]

Not only do American Buddhists share the positive view of this religion, but "Under the powerful influence of the Buddha's teaching of 'no discrimination,' women [in America] began to take and be given leadership roles, to define their own issues."[67] Buddhism in a North American context, therefore, will find more women in leadership roles and will encounter more women struggling with what Eiko Kawamura calls the horizontal dimension. In the words of another American Buddhist, Jacqueline Schwartz Mandell, "Today one may actually be fulfilled in every way, as a woman or a man, not just a non-gender being."[68] Sexuality, according to these Americans, is to be lived, not transcended.

Thus, it becomes clear that Buddhism has been understood as possessing both positive and negative attitudes towards women and women's roles. Therefore, to hear just one voice speak might give us only one perspective and a limited understanding. Once again, an example of the problems of women in dialogue has been illustrated. A Buddhist woman who believes that one must transcend the embodied self to be enlightened will have difficulty communicating with those women (Buddhist or other) who are feeling strongly about the social and religious oppression that they are experiencing.

Exactly this type of conflict occurred at the Claremont dialogue. A Zen woman master, Roshi Gesshin Prabhasa Dharma, spoke often and attempted to demonstrate that if we reflect on the way of Zen "we are beyond the discrimination of man and woman."[69] The question was posed to her about how she dealt with the issue of battered women. Her response to this concern was her description of the Buddhist teaching on suffering; suffering comes from within, from our own "battered mind. . . . When consciousness is at rest the same battering mind . . . is clear and calm, and that mind alone clearly sees reality."[70] This response illustrates a solution that requires taking leave of the outwardly physical characteristics of the problem and opting for a more introspective and transcendent solution.

From the evidence above, this attitude does not appear to be in accord with that of other American Buddhists, and this particular dialogue did not elicit a comprehensive understanding of Buddhism. Furthermore, the response created anger in many women present, and dialogue became difficult.

From the different women who represent Buddhism, we arrive at very different perspectives on the tradition itself as well as on the tradition's attitudes toward women. What, then, can we say about this tradition that has so many followers? At this point, the most we can do is to listen and hear not only the practices but the perspective of the woman speaking.

BLAMING THE "OTHER"

Feminists who view their tradition as liberating are often able to do so because their research has discovered that the root experience of the religion was egalitarian; patriarchy appeared later in history. Sometimes feminists find the fault for the religion's demise within another tradition. In other words, the "other" carries the blame for the patriarchal and misogynistic influence. This situation poses yet another problem: in order to see one's religion as liberating, one must see the other's as oppressive.

In several writings of Jewish feminists, we find the claim that Christian feminist theology is, consciously or unconsciously, anti-Semitic because Christians attribute patriarchy to Jewish influence. By examining their scriptures, Christian feminists have often found a solid rationale for their position in proving that the New Testament depicted Jesus as a feminist. In order to do so, however, it was necessary to contrast the views of Jesus with his Jewish background that was patriarchal and misogynistic. Katherina Von Kellenbach writes that "The efforts of Christian feminists were devoted to investigating the 'true meaning' or the liberating intention of the scripture."[71] Such an investigation, however,

> displays anti-Jewish tendencies: the openness towards women in the New Testament, for instance, is contrasted with the alleged sexism

and misogyny of the Jewish environment. This dualism is not fundamentally new. It is merely a continuation of traditional dichotomies
such as grace versus law, spiritual redemption versus legalism, freedom versus pharisaic hypocrisy, new versus old. A new contrast is
introduced, namely feminism versus sexism.[72]

The depiction of Jesus as a liberal male may be accurate, but, as Von
Kellenbach points out, "his feminism, that is intentional actions towards
the improvement of the position of women, depends upon a distorted
description of misogynist Jewish laws."[73]

To indicate that Christian feminists are exhibiting an anti-Jewish bias,
A. Roy Eckardt writes:

> To date, the feminist claim for [Jesus] is seldom utilized, as it could
> very well be, in order to show that Jesus' evident sympathy for women
> was typifying a moral impulse strictly within Judaism. Most often the
> claim concerning Jesus becomes a negativistic-ideological stress upon
> the faults of traditional Jewish behaviour, as against the presumed
> virtues of the central figure in Christianity.[74]

Furthermore, this anti-Jewish bias appears in the Christian feminists' explanation of the apparent misogyny in the Pauline works. Von Kellenbach
explains: "Just as the ambivalent pericopes of the Gospels are explained
as reflecting the 'stubbornness' of Israel's chauvinists with which Jesus had
to compromise, the sexism of the Pauline epistles is blamed on Paul's pharisaic education."[75]

It must be understood that Jewish writers do not deny the patriarchal
nature of Jewish tradition; they merely state that this is but one aspect of
it. Certainly, the Christian tradition has its share of male-dominated writings and practices; yet, feminists have done much work in uncovering those
little known facts that indicate that there is more egalitarianism within
Christianity than first meets the eye. The historical-critical method used by
these women as the basis of their hermeneutic must be applied to Judaism
as well. What is needed, says one Jewish feminist, Judith Plaskow, is a fair
comparison. She points out that

> the rabbis of the Mishnah and Talmud have to be compared with the
> misogyny of the Church fathers. Such a comparison would be histor-
> ically correct. It is, however, avoided. Is it avoided because the Chris-
> tian tradition would not emerge as the winner in this contest?[76]

Susannah Heschel has also criticized Christian feminists for repeating
"familiar anti-Jewish charges of earlier Christian theology."[77] She objects
to Christian women arguing that the patriarchy in their history occurred
"either through a concession to Judaism or through an unavoidable con-

tamination . . . [and interprets this type of argumentation as] the projection of Judaism as an 'other' to Christianity."[78]

Even if the Christian feminist does not take this particular position with regard to Christian exegesis, it is essential that she understand this tendency and the Jewish response to it. In dialogue, "blaming" the other for patriarchy could be as insensitive and inadequate as the stance that Christians used to take with regard to salvation. The belief that Christ is *the* way to salvation now has a counterpart in the belief that Christianity is *the* forerunner of egalitarianism. One Jewish feminist warns that by making "Judaism the scapegoat for inventing patriarchy,"[79] Christian feminists are falling "into a patriarchal trap . . . of blaming another tradition for the inadequacies of [their] own."[80] It is essential in dialogue that Christian women avoid the trap, and this is accomplished by first being aware that it exists.

At the Claremont conference of women in dialogue, participants were made aware of a similar situation between the Hindu and the Muslim women. The work on women in Hinduism attributes the patriarchy in Indian society to a number of causes, including the Brahmanic influences and the Laws of Manu (the most authoritative book of Hindu sacred law). One of the factors, however, that served to maintain Indian women in seclusion was the Muslim invasion of the twelfth century. One scholar, Katherine K. Young, writes the following about the influence:

> The segregation of the sexes became more severe after the twelfth century C.E. in those areas of the subcontinent that were under Muslim rule, especially the North, where Hindu women, already carefully controlled by or segregated from men, imitated the *purdah* of Muslim women. The consequence was that many upper caste Hindu women, already bound to the home, were further restricted so that they rarely left their residence; when they did, they covered their faces and traveled by closed carriage or palanquin.[81]

This negative Muslim influence in India was cited at the Claremont conference by a Hindu woman, Lina Gupta. While Riffat Hassan, the Muslim representative, admits the androcentric interpretation of her tradition, the accusation that this interpretation caused oppression in Hinduism, thereby mitigating the guilt of that tradition, was not well received.

On the other hand, there was a claim made regarding the negative influence of Hinduism on Hassan, a Pakistani woman. In her presentation, Gupta gave her interpretation of the goddess Sita, who was married to the king Rama and is portrayed in Hindu scriptures as the ideal woman. After Rama leaves his kingdom, his loyal wife Sita follows him only to be taken by a demon. After Rama receives his kingdom back, Sita returns, but on demand of Rama's subjects, she must prove that she has remained a chaste woman. After several more humiliations and sufferings, Sita prays to mother earth to devour her and she leaves Rama. Lina Gupta's interpretation of this story is that Sita "chose to leave even though she had a full life ahead of her."[82] Even though this goddess, according to Manu, is the perfect character of a woman in that she is long-suffering, Gupta understands her as a model of freedom. She states:

> She finally rebels ... The way I see her she has a sense of timing. In a sense she realized that there is a time and place to suffer, there is a time and place to come and there is a time and place to leave. So the time came when simple pain and suffering and endurance would not work. It is time for her to act not necessarily to react. So she left.[83]

Here we have an example of a woman, Gupta, returning to the roots of her tradition in an attempt to understand that there can be a positive position of women within them. There is, according to Gupta, a feminist interpretation of the goddess Sita.

This interpretation annoyed Riffat Hassan, who told us that "Sita is a model for actual women. When Hindu women are married, the model offered to them is, 'May you be like Sita.' "[84] But because Sita has to prove her innocence over and over again, Hassan "would hate to present her as a model for women."[85] The interesting point that concerns us here is that not only was Sita the model for Hindu women but for Hassan as well. She said, "Now I come from the same part of the world, and this is even said to Muslim women actually, that Sita is the prototype even for us."[86] Thus Hassan, a Pakistani Muslim, understands that in the backdrop of oppression that constitutes her experience, the story of the goddess Sita had a part to play.

In summary, the complexity of women in dialogue is compounded by those women who, viewing their own tradition as liberating, attribute patriarchal influences to other traditions. While traditional dialogue must guard against imperialistic claims of divine truths, so too must woman's dialogue guard against imperialistic claims of liberation.

CONCLUSION

Sometimes, when researching material on pluralism or interreligious topics, we can find a table of contents that divides the material into "The Christian Perspective," "The Buddhist Perspective," and so on. This division implies the homogeneous grouping of participants into their various traditions. However, more and more, those engaged in dialogue are aware of the diversity of views within each tradition and the danger of assuming that any one participant can represent the tradition as a whole. The problem of intrareligious differences is even more pronounced and problematic in women's dialogue. Not only are there issues of diverse doctrine and practices, but there are also those of the varying degrees of consciousness of oppression and of need for liberation. Indeed, these differences within religions can be so vast that, in some cases, women from different traditions may have more in common with one another than women from the same.

Neither can these issues be neatly classified as differences between those women who have had their consciousness raised and those who have not. If this were the case, dialogues could be simplified if they were viewed as religiously based consciousness-raising sessions. In the above analysis, women such as Monica Hellwig, Deborah Belonick, and Blu Greenberg are very aware of the need for a women's movement and indeed have been considered advocates of women's issues in religion. However, these women differ markedly from others in their respective traditions in that they maintain a more conservative stance toward the need for reform of the tradition. In Islam, also, there are women who proclaim liberation but for whom being free also means being separated from the world of men by divine decree. These women's points of view contrast to others such as those of Fatima Mernissi and Riffat Hassan, who understand equality in a much more literal sense. Thus, we see that the differences among women engaged in dialogue are not just those of the aware versus the unaware. The differences lurk much deeper and are lodged in the basic attitudes toward the meaning of equality, the nature of revelation, and the extent to which the tradition has been faithful to that revelation and has upheld or denied that equality.

The following chapters will examine specific ways in which this complexity can affect dialogue.

PART III

Considering Women's Dialogue

8

Personal Narrative
in Women's Dialogue

Considering the enormous amount of diversity that can and often does exist among women engaged in interreligious dialogue, one questions whether any communication or mutual understanding can be accomplished. This section focuses on confronting such diversity and using it to enrich dialogue, rather than to dilute it.

The first step suggested for women's dialogue may initially appear self-evident, but, on closer examination, is often ignored. The suggestion is that any meeting begin with the introduction of participants through the telling of their personal stories. While one may assume that participants in dialogue know one another, they are more likely not to be familiar with one another's cultural and religious perspectives. So much of dialogue has, until very recently, focused on the doctrinal and theological aspects of religions. Personal information has been considered irrelevant. If, however, in a women's dialogue the social issues of liberation and oppression are inseparable from the more theoretical ones, knowledge of one another's personal experiences is essential. To understand one another in relation to religion and liberation, the women must share not only their names but also their stories.

The reasons for beginning dialogue with the telling of stories are the following: (1) to create an atmosphere of trust, (2) to clarify diverse perspectives, (3) to prevent abstract and irrelevant theorizing, and (4) to discover the points of commonality and distinction.

First, an atmosphere of trust needs to be created in order that one may speak honestly and freely. It is easier to trust one whose story is known than one who is identified by name only. The establishment of trust allows one to listen to what another has to say, as well as to share who she is and what she thinks.

In Part I of this work, several points of philosophy were examined to indicate why women have not been included or listened to in the past. In most parts of the world this silence has been learned well, and simply sitting down with other women will not obliterate the sense that a woman's words are not valuable or worth the speaking. In the words of the late Nelle Morton, women must be "heard into speech."[1] But, without an atmosphere of trust created by the self-disclosure of stories, such creative listening cannot be achieved.

Listening is the key to enabling a woman to tell who she sees herself to be and not who others tell her she is. Nelle Morton's idea is "that word heard into speech creates and announces new personhood—new consciousness awakened in the human being."[2] The women in dialogue must be free to make their self-disclosures according to their own experiences and not from any prior expectations of either the women present or of the society to which they belong. Breakthroughs in self-identity need to be fostered and they can be so only in a free, non-judgmental atmosphere.

The crucial issue is that persons hear who each woman thinks she is and not who others think she is. Because the definition of woman has often been provided by tradition, myths, and images, it is important that she be free to define herself.

Thus an atmosphere of trust results in a cyclical movement of listening and speaking. Speaking personal stories yields trust, which in turn opens one to listen further. This listening, then, encourages the women to disclose the image of self that they experience rather than the image that society has imposed on them.

The second important reason for telling stories is to clarify the particular perspective represented by the participant. Chapters 6 and 7 dealt with the myriad interpretations of the concepts of oppression, feminism, and the role of religion in both of these. We examined different perspectives that are held by various women at all points on the spectrum. Unless at the beginning of the dialogue we hear these women's particular points of view and how they came to them, we are in danger of making premature assumptions. We must not assume that women representing the same religion think alike or that women from the East are of one mind regarding their role in society. As was seen in Part II, these assumptions are examples of hasty generalizations and would be setbacks, not inroads, to dialogue.

Not only will the listening to personal stories enable us to hear the diversity among women, but it will also enable us to relish and savor such diversity. In fact, as Emily Culpepper points out, this diversity will expand the meaning of feminism and liberation for us. She writes:

At its heart, Feminism promotes the radical realization that liberation is furthered by hearing each other's truths ... This process is one of the best safeguards against constructing narrow and inadequate ideas about what women need and what female freedom will involve ... Here is the emerging of an expanding Feminism that presents a rainbow of realities, for there is no standard Feminist.[3]

Although Culpepper was not specifically writing about interreligious or intercultural dialogue, her point is made more poignant when her words are applied in this area. If there is no standard feminism among women from the same culture, how much more applicable are her words when applied to a multicultural gathering.

Culpepper also relates a third reason for initiating discussion with personal stories. In a 1987 article, she writes that "including personal information is an important safeguard against feminist theory becoming too abstract and unconnected with the actual diverse situations in which women live."[4] Abstraction is a danger in interreligious dialogue because it can direct attention to the transcendent concepts that, while being the bases for the lives of many practitioners, can also be the problem for many women who find themselves excluded from either the images of the transcendent or the practices required in its worship.

One example of the tendency to use abstract thought for the basis of a commonality among the world's traditions is illustrated in John Hick's philosophy of pluralism. His observation of the variety of religions leads him to postulate that each believes in a "limitlessly greater and higher Reality beyond or within us, in relation to which or to whom is our highest good."[5] He defines such a Reality as exceeding "the reach of our earthly speech and thought. It cannot be encompassed in human concepts. It is infinite, eternal, limitlessly rich beyond the scope of our finite conceiving or experiencing."[6]

In order to understand Hick's philosophy, it is necessary to appreciate the distinction he makes between the "Real, *an sich* (in him/her/itself) and the Real as humanly experienced and thought."[7] Hick is proposing that the various religions direct their worship and commitment to the same reality that has expressed itself in varied ways. Moreover, as was pointed out in the section on feminist ethics, Hick makes the further claim that all religions involve the soteriological process of movement from self-centeredness to reality-centeredness.

What we worship and devote ourselves to, therefore, is our version of the Reality that is impossible to know in and of itself.

Philosophers of religion such as Hick, who are attempting to find an abstract idea that can be held in common by all religions, are being questioned by those who wonder whether there can be any umbrella to cover the myriad lives of actual people living each of the traditions. In an article in *Religious Studies* in 1987, Gerard Loughlin critiques Hick's work. His critique, while not specifically a feminist one, serves to illustrate the same problem that feminists are experiencing. Loughlin poses the question, "how can the world religions have a common transcendent reference, when their concepts and images of ultimate reality are so different?"[8] Even though Hick distinguishes between the way things really are and the way things are perceived, Loughlin asks if Hick can even jump to any conclusions about the way things are perceived for all religions, whether it be in terms of the nature of Reality or the nature of salvation. He expands on this point:

> We can only see things from where we are, though we can try to imagine what they look like from somewhere else ... We can see things from our own point of view, try to see them from someone else's point of view; but we cannot see them from an absolute or universally agreed point of view. If we look at the world religions from Hick's point of view then of course they will appear similarly soteriologically effective (or ineffective). But if we look at them from the point of view of someone else, then they may seem radically dissimilar.[9]

Loughlin's criticism, when applied to a women's dialogue, is reinforced and doubly effective. If he is correct in saying that "we can only see things from where we are," then how much more limited are we when we take into consideration all that has been written here about the diversity between male and female points of view. Add to this diversity the further diversity that exists among women from different cultures and different forms of oppression, and the task of arriving at an abstract commonality becomes an impossible one.

While we acknowledge that theorizing does have a place and while we do not want to deny all general principles in the dialogue, these principles should be the natural outgrowth of the particular circumstances of participants rather than an outgrowth of a previously accepted abstraction. The advantage of developing principles out of personal experiences has been illustrated by consciousness-raising groups in the United States. One lesson learned from these groups is that theories of sexual politics had to be developed from the ground up, out of personal experiences. The effect of such a method was to add to the verifiability of the theory as well as the importance of the experience.

If the political and religious are connected, then what women's groups have learned about the political can be applied to the religious as well. Thus the theories of religious pluralism would need to emerge from the analysis of personal experiences. In fact, this is exactly why Diana Eck and Devaki Jain used a case-studies format in the planning of the Harvard conference. They understood that the discussion of particular issues among participants of differing perspectives is the first step from which theoretical perspectives may, in time, emerge.[10]

Thus, the telling of personal stories is not necessarily a replacement for the theories of religious pluralism, but rather a new starting point in their development. The advantage of this method is, in Culpepper's words, the establishment "of a female train of thought tracing a line of thinking formulated by women."[11] Considering how androcentric the most obvious of our thought patterns have been and the unique nature of women's experience, we can appreciate the need for a female "train of thought."

Still another advantage of the personal story remains. Only in the telling of stories can persons discover the points of commonality and distinction among themselves. Again Emily Culpepper asserts, "This [storytelling] has been and continues to be one of the surest means of genuinely discovering the connections among women."[12] In Part II we explored the very real possibility that women from different cultures and religions may have more in common than women from the same geographical areas and faith traditions. The only way such a phenomenon can become known is through the telling of stories. In the responses and feelings conveyed in story form, experiences of liberation or oppression can often be portrayed more adequately and understood more fully by the other. For example, on the surface, the liberated Christian woman could hardly identify with, or see a relationship to, the Muslim woman who understands herself as liberated by the message of the Qur'an. The experience of hearing this woman's story, however, can create a new and invigorating consciousness.

Just as similarities in life stories are more readily discernible, so also are the differences. However, when differences are merely known abstractly outside of the context of a person's story, they are more likely to be divisive. In her work, Culpepper discovered that "As more and more stories unfold, women are summoning up tremendous courage to face the divisions among us that fracture our lives and to explore what separations may not have been previously questioned."[13]

In conclusion, the telling of personal stories, which at first may seem self-evident and unnecessary, is essential for women's interreligious dialogue. Sarah Cunningham's words in *Women of Faith in Dialogue* express this point well:

All our stories prepare us for this new chapter in our lives, for leaping into the unknown dimensions of interreligious dialogue. Only as we move into such a dialogue can we find out what the future holds for such a venture. We can expect new questions, new knowings, new levels of trust in one another, new affirmations of faith.[14]

9

The Constructive Use of Conflict

The telling of personal stories alone certainly will not achieve the goal of dialogue and bring about mutual understanding and growth. This assumption would be quite simplistic. Nor can any specific formula be proposed that will insure a dialogue's success. One fact can be said with some degree of certainty, however: women's interreligious dialogue is sure to involve some conflict. Therefore, any realistic study of dialogue must consider ways to approach such conflict and make possible its resolution.

First, a preliminary disclaimer is necessary. While guidelines and methodology are needed, no single theory can be applied to so many diverse and complex human interactions. Because each person is unique and the dynamics between individuals can never be totally predicted, all general comments must be considered as mere suggestions and not as definitive rules. The Islamic feminist scholar Riffat Hassan, who has herself been a faithful and long-time participant in interreligious dialogue, issues this warning in an article in *Religion and Intellectual Life*. She writes:

> I do not find theorizing or strategizing *about* dialogue and being in dialogue to be at all the same thing ... The dialogue of life which emerges out of the processes of life is not a contrived matter. It arises "naturally" as it were from the interaction, positive and negative, obvious and subtle, verbal and nonverbal, between various peoples or persons.[1]

Understanding that theories cannot be universally applicable, the following comments are offered as recollections of some helpful strategies that, however vague, must remain in a woman's consciousness as she approaches the dialogue table.

HELPFUL STRATEGIES

Conflict is one of those important communication topics that has been receiving much attention by those studying gender issues. What happens when two or more participants disagree and find themselves faced with a seemingly irremovable difference? In one debriefing session held after the Claremont conference, a communications instructor explained that in the secular world, men are generally more comfortable with confrontation than are women. Indeed, one text on gender and communication states that "Many females find the argumentative style not only difficult to use, but inhibiting when it is used against them."[2] American feminists are also raising the issue of the double standard with regard to anger. For men anger is not only justifiable but a sign of conviction and strength, whereas for women, it is a taboo labeling them as emotional and irrational. Hence, many women are usually demure or depressed rather than angry.

In interreligious dialogue, however, the experience of my colleagues and the literature suggest that the situation is just the opposite. In the dialogues of male participants, religious matters were discussed with great civility and mutual agreement, even in the midst of ideological challenges.

This does not appear to be the case in those dialogues that have taken place among women. In these situations, women seem to be open enough to disagree, challenge, and contradict. These moments lead to conflict, which at times becomes quite intense. I suggest that the reason for the discrepancy among men's and women's dialogue is that, in the areas of religion and philosophy, women have been silenced or ignored for so long that when they dialogue among themselves, they take the opportunity to express their anger and to deal with it.[3] However, the expression of anger and the conflict that results can potentially destroy a feeling of trust and good will so necessary in dialogue. For this reason, we will examine some advantages of expressing anger and conflict and the constructive use of both.

The first factor that must be recognized is that conflict does not always have to end in agreement. Its very existence can be an asset rather than a liability in interreligious dialogue. This point is clearly made by Maurice Friedman in a 1987 issue of *Horizons*. He is responding to Paul Knitter's criticisms of his article "Dialogue of Touchstones," in which Knitter accuses him of not saying enough about "the possibility of a real clash . . . , of mutual incompatibilities, of possible ruptures in the dialogue."[4] Knitter reminds his readers of the "suggestions of liberation theologians . . . that . . . our Community of Otherness can grow not only through mutual confirmation but also through mutual confrontation, even conflict."[5]

Friedman replies that he is comfortable living with opposites, and he refuses the temptation to try to convert the dilemmas to agreements. He says:

> I do not assume that the goal of dialogue is agreement or that dialogue is only of value if it leads to agreement . . . but oppositeness all too often crystallizes into opposition . . . The only perspective from which we can find comfort in the face of such . . . conflict is the Talmudic

approach that holds that "every conflict that takes place for the sake of heaven endures." This is completely contrary to Aristotelian logic with its assumption that a statement and its opposite cannot both be truth. To say that both sides will endure does not mean that eventually one will be proved right and the other wrong. The knowledge that the other also witnesses for [her] "touchstone of reality" from where [she] stands can enable us to confirm the other in [her] truth even while opposing [her].[6]

The key issue here is respect for the other and trust that the opposing position is being held as a result of the experience of the participant. Experiences cannot be denied, and neither can one's interpretation of them. As Friedman writes, "I can open myself to what the other says; I can recognize the witness of the other even in opposing it; and I can reaffirm my own witness in dialogue with that of the other."[7] This trust that the recounting of experiences is genuine, regardless of how foreign it may seem, is a strategic point that makes listening possible. This experience of being heard affirms one's worth and identity. It also allows one the freedom to risk being open and even self-critical. Friedman writes, "Sometimes the strongest opposition is more confirming by far than someone who defends your right to your opinion but does not take it seriously."[8]

The second point to be considered is that conflict, besides being a respectful recognition that the other is different from me, can also be a source of growth and insight. Conflict can reveal key issues at the heart of some of the wider problems confronting our world. This role of conflict was experienced by the conveners of the Harvard Conference, Diana Eck and Devaki Jain. They write:

> It is precisely conflict that reveals the fault lines where world understanding cracks ... The insight we gained during our week together was that conflict was not only possible, but constructive, in the context of an emerging community.[9]

As with Eck's and Jain's experience, some of the most intense and enlightening moments of the Claremont conference involved conflict. Riffat Hassan challenged Lina Gupta in her interpretation of the Hindu Goddess Sati: how can Sati possibly serve as a model of liberation? Drorah Setel, a Jewish feminist, brought a heightened awareness in her very direct challenge to the group to be conscious of the use of words: for example, did we really mean Christian when we said Western? And many women present were angered at the Roshi's solutions to ending the battering of women. Can the practice of Zen and the achievement of enlightenment really adequately respond to so many injustices?

These challenges and the discussion they provoked caused the participants to touch the real problems that different traditions have with one another. The confrontations evoked the realization that they must be addressed rather than quieted or dismissed as insignificant. Opposing viewpoints must be listened to, questioned, and explained until clarified. Only through this type of ardent effort will problems be resolved rather than brushed aside or ignored, only to surface in unexpected and undesired forms later. Only when feelings of oppression or injustice are heard will anger be assuaged and confrontation be constructive rather than destructive.

Focusing on specific conflict situations, we notice one that seems to be unique to women's interreligious dialogue. Previous sections examined the diversity of women's views of oppression and of the liberating power of their religion. When women who find the doctrines of their religion liberating meet with women who are in oppressed situations, the danger is that the solutions of the former will be offered to solve the problems of the latter. The difficulty here is that while oppression must be listened to, solutions must be given cautiously or, better yet, not given at all. We cannot presume to know the answers to other peoples' problems, especially people from other cultures and religious traditions.

Examples of the problem occurred at the Claremont conference. As mentioned earlier, when the Roshi attempted to solve the problem of battered woman by appealing to the practice of Zen, the Western women reacted with conflict and anger. Similar reactions also resulted when Pravajika Bhaktiprana, an American-born nun of the Ramakrishna sect, spoke of the divine within the human soul that is manifested in the four yogas. She explained that all women are the symbol of the divine mother and all men are called son. This was a difficult concept to grasp, much less to accept, when many women were feeling deeply the oppression of patriarchal structures. From these examples, one can conclude that when a woman in dialogue offers an ideological solution from within one tradition for a particular problem experienced by women from another, conflict could ensue.

The problem here is not so much that the Roshi or Pravajika had not known oppression or injustice, but rather that their method of dealing with it could only be explained but could not be offered as a solution for another's situation. Again we meet the dual problem presented by women in dialogue. Not only are there differences between those aware and those unaware of being oppressed, but there are also different perspectives on the means of liberation. For some the solution is Zen meditation, for others, Vendanta ritual; or the invocation of Christ; or the Goddess. These problems make the dialogue of women full of complexities not yet met in the traditional male-oriented situation.

One way in which both problems and solutions can be heard by all and discussed fruitfully is to structure one session in such a way that the discussion focuses on practices that oppress and traditions that liberate. These can be faced in a very straightforward manner without creating an impasse in the dialogue. In one of the planning sessions for the Claremont conference, June O'Connor of the University of California at Riverside suggested that it would be advantageous for each participant to identify the positive and negative impact that her religion had on her life as a woman.

Two things can be learned in such a structure. First, one can discover factors that constitute a negative situation for each participant. Thus, the meaning of oppression as well as the differences between the fact of oppression and awareness of it can be explored. Second, the views of religion as oppressor or liberator can be expressed. I propose, therefore, that a possible solution to the conflicts that arise when one participant offers to solve the problems of another would be to ask two questions: (1) How has your religion helped you develop your identity as a woman? and (2) How has your religion hindered or confined your growth as a woman?

The first question, regarding the positive aspects, often elicits responses that refer to the original intentions of the founders of particular traditions. Many women cite the opinion that in its pristine form their religion is basically egalitarian. Sharing these aspects forces the participants to hear how others achieve a positive view of self from being a devotee of a particular tradition. The Roshi could then speak of the Buddhist experience of emptiness in which all differences disappear. Lina Gupta could relate the stories of the Hindu goddesses that give her both a precedent and the strength to follow that precedent. Riffat Hassan could speak of the conclusion of her Qur'anic exegesis, revealing the true intention of the prophet. Within these explanations are contained the answers to each woman's method of coping with her situation.

The second question, concerning negative aspects, might deal with the specific problems that women experience and areas in which change must take place. Pravajika Bhaktiprana spoke about the egalitarian philosophy of the Vedanta society. Yet at the same time she mentioned the paternalistic attitude held by the Indian swami towards the American women with whom he associates. This type of problematic—the coexistence of both egalitarianism and sexism—was a situation to which women around the table could relate. Therefore, a good springboard for dialogue was established.

David Tracy seems to refer both to positive and negative aspects when he writes of the attitudes demanded by interreligious conversation. These attitudes are explained "as both rootedness in a tradition and the self-transcendence of critical reflection ... all our best critical reflections are needed if the conversation is to prove a genuine conversation."[10] By "rootedness," Tracy refers to the connectedness that participants have with their tradition. For women in dialogue, this connectedness presupposes the positive aspects of the religion that attract her.

The "self-transcendent critical reflection" spoken of by Tracy implies that women need to be able to see not only who they are but also who they can and want to be. In this light, they must examine the ways in which they understand forces that constrain them. They must also criticize their tradition if necessary. I understand these criticisms to be the content of the negative aspects of one's religion. Sharing negative aspects, such as the problems that women have with the patriarchal structures or practices, can bring together those women who have struggled to change their own religions. Their coming together can enable them to continue the task.

Dividing the content of dialogue into positive and negative aspects makes possible the analysis of a tradition not only from the individual woman's perspective but also from the perspective of society as a whole. It is important for participants to realize that their own tradition as well as others' have acted both to liberate and to oppress them in social situations at various times in history. Some of the greatest atrocities as well as some of the greatest social reforms have been done in the name of religion. Christianity was used to legitimize feudalism, capitalism, and racial discrimination. Hinduism was used to perpetuate the practice of caste discrimination and untouchability. The Bhakti movement in Hinduism, however, challenged the discriminatory caste system just as the liberation theology of Christianity is challenging the unjust political and economic status quo.

In conclusion, evaluating positive and negative influences of religion on one's identity as a woman, has been suggested not to eliminate the existence of conflict among participants, but to allow the conflict to be enriching and informative. Channeling both positive and negative views of religion into two direct questions that address persons in their own religious contexts can serve to avoid roadblocks in discussion. Because so many different perspectives will confront each other in so many different combinations, one needs to structure the discussion in such a way that participants will not be swatting at invisible flies or passing one another in linguistic elevators. The division of the discussion in this way can serve to facilitate an effective interreligious dialogue.

Conclusion

Implications of Women's Dialogue

If women meet apart from their male counterparts, and if they encounter and meet the challenges discussed in the previous section, what will happen? Looking at the limited number of such dialogues that have taken place, examining their repercussions, and looking at the future possibilities for women in dialogue, it appears that there could be a ripple effect of implications. Immediate effects would be felt by the women participants themselves. As their meetings grow more numerous and more widely known, and as their discussions are recorded in a body of literature, the wider community of women, both in and out of academia, would be affected by their work. The long-range goal of the endeavor is a dialogue in which women and men would participate equally. If and when this occurs, the present dialogue could be transformed and understanding could exist across religious and cultural lines and across gender lines as well.

The ripple effect consists then in this: as the rock of women's dialogue is thrown out, the waters are moved first for the women themselves, then for the international women's community, and finally, for the community of women and men engaged in the task of mutual understanding. A prediction of such a disturbance of the waters was made by Harvey Cox. He foresees that "when women become full partners, the interreligious dialogue will change so much that what is now going on will be regarded as only an insufficient and misleading beginning."[1]

IMPLICATIONS FOR WOMEN THEMSELVES

Engaging in interreligious dialogue involves risks. Anyone who participates in a genuine exchange must be prepared to have his or her most cherished values and entire world view challenged. If it is not changed, it will at least experience nuances to some degree. For women, however, the added risk is confronting the fact of oppression—one's own and that of others.

As was pointed out in Part II of this study, many, but not necessarily all, women engaging in dialogue have been the subjects of oppression. Their awareness of such is present in varying degrees. However, when one less aware meets with other women suffering oppression, the sense of what is happening to oneself is intensified. After hearing the stories of her sisters, the woman who does not necessarily see her situation as oppressive runs the risk of becoming aware that it is, and this is a very painful experience.

Robin Morgan had a similar experience when she was editing one of the first works of the women's movement, *Sisterhood Is Powerful.* While she does not claim to be speaking cross-culturally, she does describe her feelings as a North American in these poignant words:

> It makes you very sensitive — raw, even — this consciousness ... everything seems to barrage your aching brain, which has fewer and fewer protective defenses to screen such things out. You begin to see how all-pervasive a thing is sexism — the definition of and discrimination against half the human species by the other half. Once started, the realization is impossible to stop, and it packs a daily wallop.[2]

At this point in conclusion, I am going to follow some advice given by Carol Christ in her *Laughter of Aphrodite.* She urges the use of personal story because she believes "we must risk writing personally if we are to be true to what we know at the deepest levels of our being and to the insights with which we create feminist theology."[3] In keeping with this injunction and my own suggestion in Chapter 9 of this work, I risk writing personally.

In the late sixties and early seventies several of my male friends were ordained to the Catholic priesthood. I remember the rejoicing and celebrations that I shared with them on those profound occasions. In 1974 I became very involved in the Women's Ordination Movement, which brought me together with women who also wished to be ordained. After sharing community with them and studying the subject so as to be a qualified spokesperson, I attended another ordination. Again, several of my friends were on the altar laying hands on the head of the ordinands. At that moment, the injustice of being excluded from the brotherhood on the sole basis of my sex hit me in such a dramatic way that what was expected to be a joyous occasion turned out to be one of extreme pain. When one of my priest friends said laughingly, "Well, Maura, some day that will be you," tears came to my eyes and he knew what had happened. I was never again able to attend a service without experiencing the pain of that day.

This story is offered as an example of what can happen when women share stories, hopes, and challenges. It is important to understand that this kind of awareness can occur at any stage of one's liberation. At the time of the above incident, I thought of myself as part of the women's movement. Years later, when I considered myself a more "advanced" member of the women's movement, one of my fellow doctoral students made me aware of my use of male pronouns for God. Again, another turning point in awareness. These experiences serve to illustrate two points: (1) at whatever stage a woman is in her awareness of oppression, there is room for increased consciousness, hence more pain; and (2) poignant moments of sharp awareness are not reserved for those women who are professional theologians and from whom we have heard many conversion experiences, such as the Mary Dalys, the Carol Christs and the Rosemary Ruethers. They occur to anyone who sincerely seeks to understand others, and hence herself, by entering into dialogue with her sisters.

Another implication of women's dialogue for the participants is an awareness not only of being oppressed but also of being the oppressor. In an earlier section of this work, Sharon Welch, who authored *Communities of Resistance and Solidarity: A Feminist Theology of Liberation*, was quoted. Her words need repeating because of their import. She writes:

> I cannot be at all sure that my own understanding of humanity is not limited by the acceptance of some unseen form of oppression. Just as slavery and the treatment of women were for centuries not even recognized by sensitive theologians and people of faith as oppressive, it is possible that my thought and actions share in the perpetuation of as yet unrecognized forms of oppression.[4]

Women talking to women of other religions, other cultures, or other awareness levels, run the risk of being made aware of their possible negative effect on others.

In March of 1988 I attended a lecture given by Susannah Heschel on Jewish Feminism in which she was particularly critical of certain aspects of Christian theology that she considered to be anti-Jewish. In defense, I explained some of my own education with regard to these issues. After a lengthy exchange between us, I realized that the issue of Jewish women's identity was not being recognized in my perspective, but was being interpreted through a Christian framework. This type of consciousness raising is also painful because it is quite humbling to see yourself in the very position of those who are the subject of your anger.

In summary, women who engage in interreligious dialogue have the enriching experience of encountering sisters from all places. They are able to acquire a new self-knowledge born out of viewing themselves from a perspective of such diversity. However, they also run a great risk. Women in dialogue face two difficult awarenesses: (1) the awareness of their own oppression at new and deeper levels than previously realized, and (2) the recognition that there have been subtle and often unrecognized actions on their part that have caused others to be oppressed. Both of these points are difficult to hear and can provoke pain, anger, and defensiveness. Both of these conflicting situations, however, can lead to a self-understanding and an understanding of the other that most likely could not be arrived at in any other way.

IMPLICATIONS FOR THE INTERNATIONAL WOMEN'S COMMUNITY

The implications of a women's interreligious dialogue for the international women's community are threefold. First, women will have a greater awareness and appreciation of diversity among themselves; second, there will arise the need for women to reflect on and write about their conversation; and third, women will be more prepared to act for social change. Through dialogue and literature, women will be able to communicate their growing consciousness of themselves and others and their experiences of similarities and differences with one another. In this situation of interreligious dialogue, communication is empowerment.

The meaning of concepts such as oppression, liberation, and feminism cannot be assumed. Because of the issues discussed in the second part of this study, the women who come together to dialogue must forsake a preconceived notion of a specific unifying factor to launch the discussion. One cannot assume that all of the women gathered have either been oppressed or have seen their religion as excluding them in any way. Such assumptions have often been made at previous women's dialogues. In the edited papers of the conference at Harvard Divinity School in 1983, we read about the hope of a "common foundation for social change."[5] In her book recounting a meeting of Christian, Jewish, and Muslim women, Virginia Ramey Mollenkott writes that "common experiences of women run through all traditions."[6] However, after understanding the enormous diversity that exists among women of various cultures and religions, the women's community must face the possibility that they might not find, in every meeting, a common foundation for change or any common experiences. The mutual respect for the uniqueness of each woman may be the only fruit of any one particular meeting. What must be learned by women in the face of such enormous diversity is patience—a wild patience[7] that acknowledges that while personal revelation and reflection is the most effective way to coalesce toward change, it is also the most time consuming.

The thoughts of David Lochhead, while not written specifically for a woman's dialogue, are particularly germane to this situation. He understands that one need not hold any anxiety about the concrete accomplishments of any specific interreligious dialogue, since dialogue, if understood as genuine listening and honest sharing, can be an end in itself.

> A truly dialogical relationship has no other purpose than itself. Dialogue is the end of dialogue . . . To attempt dialogue for what we can get out of it is too egocentric an attitude . . . one compromises the dialogical relationship if one attempts to justify it by its results.[8]

If this be the case and if the coming together to dialogue is an end rather than a means, then what about the talk of a global mutual understanding and world peace, those lofty ideals with which this study began? Can we have any hopes for practical results, or does the very diversity render women powerless to effect any improvement of oppressive situations? Does it prevent women from rejoicing in one another's liberation and self-identity?

Dialogue is a commitment. The more one engages in it, the greater is the perspective and the goal. Initially, we must dedicate ourselves to the task at hand: the sharing with the women whom we wish to come to know. Only after dialogues happen and happen among many women in many places can mutual understanding be realized. Only through dialogue can we learn one another's needs, the existence and extent of a culture's oppressive practices, the woman's reaction to those practices, and the most effective ways to end them.

Women who engage in such a dialogue sometimes are criticized for talking too much and acting too little to oppose the real evils of oppression and exploitation that are crushing so many women throughout the world. The type of dialogue envisioned in these pages is not an exercise in futile relativism often passed off as the virtue of tolerance. Nor is it viewed as an alternative for those considered lacking either the courage or the opportunity to engage in political activity. Rather, it is an honest endeavor that seeks to discover, through conversation, the reality of oppression and to separate that reality from what is truly culturally relative. While the deeds of rape and murder may be essentially evil, and while women may be united in their attempts to obliterate them, there are many situations that lie between rape and freedom that are not so easily discernible. Furthermore, the social evils that give rise to the rape and murder vary, and with differences in sources come differences in solutions. Dialogue is also an attempt to learn these solutions for changing oppressive situations.

The results of this study indicate that women must continue to meet, and that the meetings must be held more frequently and more inclusively. Not only must the meetings take place; people attending them must be debriefed; the ideas surfaced must be critically reflected upon, and recorded. In this reflection women will be able to discover the advantages and the value of their international community. Then, when women from all parts of the world achieve the heightened awareness of themselves and their sisters, action will be possible because they will be empowered with the courage to move and the knowledge of where to go.

IMPLICATIONS FOR THE COMMUNITY OF WOMEN AND MEN IN DIALOGUE

Women coming together, women strengthening their solidarity in community, women reflecting and writing about their identity and experience — all these phenomena cannot be ignored by the larger community of women and men. These situations must have an impact on what until now has been a predominantly male enterprise. In the philosophical consideration of pluralism, should not gender be the most basic form of pluralism? Is not the most fundamental plurality one in which men and women can exist as equals in all aspects of their mutually shared lives—religious, social, and familial?

Literature on pluralism and interreligious dialogue written by male theologians reflects cultural and religious differences. After we recognize the androcentrism of philosophy that has contributed to the exclusion of women, and after we have listened to the uniqueness of women's experiences throughout the world, the existing works appear inadequate. For example, when John Hick acknowledges cultural differences to develop his philosophy of pluralism, he writes of being human "in one or other of the various concrete ways of being human which constitute the cultures of the earth. There is a Chinese way of being human, an African way, an Arab way, a European way, or ways and so on."⁹ He appears to neglect the important fact that within each of these ways there exists a more fundamental difference—that is, a male way of being human and a female way. How would this affect his philosophy of pluralism?

Likewise, Gordon Kaufman, in his essay on religious diversity, asks the question, "How, in all our diversity, can we humans learn to live together fruitfully, productively and in peace in today's complexly interconnected world?"¹⁰ Kaufman is also speaking of religious diversity without considering the added complexity of the gender diversity within it.

In his book *Toward a Universal Theology of Religion*, Leonard Swidler states:

> Interreligious, interideological dialogue operates in three areas: the practical, where we collaborate to help humanity; the "spiritual," where we attempt to experience the partner's religion or ideology "from within"; and the cognitive, where we seek understanding and truth.¹¹

Yet, while Swidler understands that helping humanity means marching together at Selma,¹² would he also see the necessity of protesting with the women who are excluded from the Catholic priesthood? Have male Christian participants in dialogue attempted to experience religion as much from within a women's perspective as from within a Buddhist's perspective? Unless these implications are as evident in Swidler's remarks as are others, then the dialogue is not fundamentally pluralistic; the comments of these theologians fall short of their richer and more comprehensive meaning. The dimensions of the human community need to be expanded in all their visions to include the woman, her voice, her story, and her lessons. She must join together in the teaching and the learning so that the human community may genuinely grow and develop to its full potential.

A complete description of a utopian community of men and women in dialogue is impossible to envision at this point. Yet, excitement grows in knowing of areas yet to be explored and results yet to be imagined. When men and women enter into an open dialogue as equal participants, the results could be revolutionizing.

In the words of theologian David Lochhead,

> dialogue is not so much a process of sharing truth as it is of discovering it. . . . The most significant way in which truth is discovered in dialogue is when I and my dialogue partner together discover something neither of us had known before.[13]

New truths will be discovered that are beyond those already known: truths about men and about women, about their relationship to one another and to God. If these words are taken seriously, we have yet uncharted waters to explore, and this kind of adventure is exciting. Some of this excitement has been captured by Ursula King:

> I can see an interdependence of religious, social and sexual evolution which will affect the notion of God or the Ultimate, our understanding of human persons, as well as the understanding and practice of the autonomy of the acting subject. All three bear the seeds of a new religion, a new spirituality, and a new mysticism.[14]

A noble feat indeed, but one within our possibilities if we have the courage to acknowledge our finitude, the love to embrace the other's differences, and the perseverance to settle for nothing less than a renewed face of the earth.

Notes

INTRODUCTION

1. John Hick, *Problems of Religious Pluralism* (New York: St. Martin's Press, 1985), p. 30.

2. Of the literature on interreligious dialogue that was researched, the earliest that mentioned the presence of women was in 1977 at the Geneva meeting of the World Council of Churches. Since then, women were included in consultations in India on "Authority of the Religions and the Status of Women" in 1985, and two women attended the Claremont Conference on interreligious dialogue in 1986. Other works regarding interreligious dialogue do not mention women except if the dialogue consists of women only and is dedicated to their concerns.

CHAPTER 1

1. J. Paul Rajashekar, "Dialogue with People of Other Faiths and Ecumenical Theology," *Current Dialogue* (December 1987): 13.

2. Linda Gardiner, "Can This Discipline Be Saved? Feminist Theory Challenges Mainstream Philosophy," Working Paper No. 118, Wellesley College Center for Research on Women, Wellesley, MA, 1983.

3. Susan C. Bourque and Donna Robinson Divine, *Women Living Change* (Philadelphia: Temple University Press, 1985), p. 2.

4. Sheila Ruth, "Methodocracy, Misogyny, and Bad Faith: The Response of Philosophy," in *Men's Studies Modified*, ed. Dale Spender (Oxford: Pergamon Press, 1981), p. 46.

5. Wilfred Cantwell Smith, *Towards a World Theology* (Philadelphia: The Westminster Press, 1981), pp. 49–50.

6. Wilfred Cantwell Smith, *Meaning and End of Religion* (New York: New American Library, 1964), p. 141.

7. Raimundo Panikkar, *The Unknown Christ of Hinduism*, revised and enlarged edition (Maryknoll: Orbis Books, 1981), p. 43.

8. John Hick, "On Grading Religions," *Religious Studies* 17 (December 1981): 456.

9. Ruth, p. 46.

10. Sandra Harding, "Is Gender a Variable in Conceptions of Rationality? A Survey of Issues," in *Beyond Domination: New Perspectives on Women and Philosophy*, ed. Carol C. Gould (Totowa: Rowman & Allanheld, 1983), pp. 48–49.

11. Penelope Brown and L. Jordanova, "Oppressive Dichotomies: The Nature/ Culture Debate," in *The Changing Experience of Women*, eds. Elizabeth Whitelegg et al. (Oxford: Martin Robertson, 1982), p. 390.

12. Ibid.

13. Marian Lowe, "The Dialectic of Biology and Culture," in *Woman's Nature*, eds. Marian Lowe and Ruth Hubbard (New York: Pergamon Press, 1983), p. 56.

14. Jean Grimshaw, *Philosophy and Feminist Thinking*, (Minneapolis: University of Minnesota Press, 1986), p. 132.

15. Alison M. Jaggar, "Human Biology in Feminist Theory: Sexual Equality Reconsidered," in *Beyond Domination: New Perspectives on Women and Philosophy*, ed. Coral C. Gould (Totowa: Rowman and Allanheld, 1983), pp. 36–37.

16. Ibid.

17. Ibid., p. 38.

18. Brown and Jordanova, p. 391.

19. Genevieve Lloyd, *The Man of Reason: 'Male' and 'Female' in Western Philosophy* (London: Methuen and Co., 1984), pp. 49–50.

20. Ibid., p. 69.

21. Immanuel Kant, "Foundations of the Metaphysics of Morals," in *Kant: Selections*, ed. Lewis White Beck (New York: Macmillan Publishing Co., 1988), pp. 245, 252.

22. Ibid., p. 252.

23. Lawrence L. Blum, "Kant's and Hegel's Moral Rationalism: A Feminist Perspective," *Canadian Journal of Philosophy* 12 (June 1982): 288, 296.

24. Ibid., p. 290.

25. Arnulf Zweig, "Introduction," in *Kant: Philosophical Correspondence*, ed. and trans. Arnulf Zweig (Chicago: University of Chicago Press, 1967), p. 26.

26. Lloyd, p. 103.

27. Grimshaw, p. 132.

28. Nancy Tuana, "A Reply to Laura Purdy," *Hypatia: A Journal of Feminist Philosophy* 1 (Spring 1986): 175.

29. Caroline Whitbeck, "A Different Reality: Feminist Ontology," in Gould, *Beyond Domination*, p. 76.

30. Tuana, p. 175.

CHAPTER 2

1. Leonard Swidler, "Interreligious and Interideological Dialogue: The Matrix for All Systematic Reflection Today," in *Toward a Universal Theology of Religion*, ed. Leonard Swidler (Maryknoll: Orbis Books, 1988), p. 12.

2. Sandra Harding, *The Science Question in Feminism* (Ithaca: Cornell University Press, 1986), p. 138.

3. Ibid., p. 141.

4. Sandra Harding and Merrill B. Hintikka, eds., *Discovering Reality: Feminist Perspectives on Epistemology, Metaphysics, Methodology, and Philosophy of Science* (Boston: D. Reidel Pub. Co., 1983), p. x.

5. Dale Spender, *For the Record: The Making and Meaning of Feminist Knowledge* (London: The Women's Press, 1985), p. 28.

6. Carol McMillan, *Women, Reason and Nature: Some Philosophical Problems with Feminism* (Princeton: Princeton University Press, 1982), p. 42.

7. Ibid., p. 12.

8. Ibid., p. 41.

9. Harding, p. 199.

10. Evelyn Fox Keller, "Gender and Science," in *Twenty Questions: An Introduction to Philosophy*, eds. G. Lee Bowie, Meridith W. Michaels, Robert C. Solomon (San Diego: Harcourt Brace Jovanovich, 1988), p. 94.

11. Ibid.

12. Ibid.

13. Ibid., p. 97.

14. Ibid.

15. G. van der Leeuw, *Religion in Essence and Manifestation*, vol. 1, trans. J. E. Turner (New York: Harper & Row, 1963), p. iii.

16. See Sharon D. Welch, *Communities of Resistance and Solidarity: A Feminist Theology of Liberation* (Maryknoll: Orbis Books, 1985), p. 28.

17. Ibid.

18. Ibid.

19. Thomas B. Ommen, "Relativism, Objectivism, and Theology," *Horizons* 13 (1986): 301.

20. Anne Seller, "Realism versus Relativism: Towards a Politically Adequate Epistemology," in *Feminist Perspectives in Philosophy*, eds. Morwenna Griffiths and Margaret Whitford (Indianapolis: Indiana University Press, 1988), p. 170.

21. Ibid., p. 179.

22. Ommen, p. 302.

23. Seller, p. 180.

24. Ommen, p. 305.

25. Welch, p. 84.

26. Ibid., pp. 85–86.

27. Ibid., p. 87.

28. Ommen, p. 305.

CHAPTER 3

1. L. Shannon Jung, "Feminism and Spatiality: Ethics and the Recovery of a Hidden Dimension," *Journal of Feminist Studies in Religion* 4 (Spring 1988): 59.

2. Lloyd, *Man of Reason*, p. 103.

3. Grimshaw, pp. 65ff.

4. Ibid., pp. 187–9.

5. Ibid., p. 189.

6. Ibid.

7. Rosi Braidotti, "Ethics Revisited: Women and/in Philosophy," in *Feminist Challenges: Social and Political Theory*, eds. Carole Pateman and Elizabeth Gross (Boston: Northeastern University Press, 1986), p. 44.

8. Grimshaw, *Philosophy and Feminist Thinking*, pp. 198–99.

9. Ibid., p. 189.

10. Carol Gilligan, *In a Different Voice* (Cambridge: Harvard University Press, 1982), pp. 62–63.

11. In Grimshaw, p. 192.

12. Josephine Donovan, *Feminist Theory: The Intellectual Traditions of American Feminism* (New York: Ungar Publishing Co., 1987), p. 176.

13. Robb, "A Framework for Feminist Ethics," p. 232.

14. Ruth L. Smith, "Feminism and the Moral Subject," in *Women's Consciousness, Women's Conscience*, ed. Barbara Hilkert Andolsen et al. (San Francisco: Harper & Row, 1985), p. 241.

15. Valerie Saiving, "The Human Situation: A Feminine View," in *Womenspirit Rising*, ed. Carol Christ and Judith Plaskow (New York: Harper & Row, 1979), p. 37.

16. Ibid., p. 39.

17. Jean Baker Miller, *Toward a New Psychology of Women*, 2nd ed. (Boston: Beacon Press, 1986), p. 50.

18. Ibid.

19. Saiving, p. 41.

20. John Hick, "The Non-Absoluteness of Christianity," in *The Myth of Christian Uniqueness*, p. 23.

21. Ibid.

22. Susan Nelson Dunfee, "The Sin of Hiding: A Feminist Critique of Reinhold Neibuhr's Account of the Sin of Pride," *Soundings* 65 (Fall 1982): 316.

23. This interpretation of male theology was further elaborated in discussions with colleague L. J. Tess Tessier.

24. Paula Cooey, "The Power of Transformation and the Transformation of Power," *Journal of Feminist Studies in Religion* 1 (Spring 1985):26.

25. Hick, "On Grading Religions," *Religious Studies* 17 (December 1981): 467.

26. Saiving, p. 37.

27. Cooey, p. 25.

28. Ibid., p. 30.

29. John Hick, *An Interpretation of Religion* (New Haven: Yale University Press, 1989), p. 53.

30. Ibid., p. 54.

31. Saiving, p. 37.

32. Hick, *Interpretation*, p. 54.

33. Elaboration of this argument emerged after discussions with colleagues Christa McNerney and Sandra MacNevin-Xu. Further development was done by June O'Connor in a paper delivered in Claremont, California, April 7, 1989, entitled "Sin and Salvation from a Feminist Perspective."

34. Mary Daly, *Pure Lust: Elemental Feminist Philosophy* (Boston: Beacon Press, 1984), p. 105n.

35. Emily Erwin Culpepper, "Philosophia in a Feminist Key: Revolt of the Symbols," Ph.D. dissertation, Harvard University, 1983, p. 107.

36. Ibid., p. 106.

37. Hick, *Interpretation*, p. 54.

38. June O'Connor, "Sin and Salvation from a Feminist Perspective: A Response to C. Robert Mesle and John Hick," paper delivered in Claremont, California, April 7, 1989, p. 7.

39. Grimshaw, p. 224.

CHAPTER 4

1. Denise Lardner Carmody and John Tully Carmondy, *Ways to the Center*, 2nd ed. (Belmont: Wadsworth Publishing Co., 1984), p. 343.

2. Conversation with Riffat Hassan, Sept. 30, 1989.

3. Sartaz Aziz, "Recollection of a Muslim Woman," *Women of Power* (Fall 1986): 53.

4. Riffat Hassan, "Messianism and Islam," *Journal of Ecumenical Studies* 22 (Spring 1985):263.

5. Ellen S. Sidor, ed., *A Gathering of Spirit: Women Teaching in American Buddhism* (Cumberland: Primary Point Press, 1987), p. 2.

6. This definition is taken from Nancy Wilson Ross, *Buddhism: A Way of Life and Thought* (New York: Vintage Books, 1981), p. 95.

7. Lenore Friedman, ed., *Meetings With Remarkable Women* (Boston: Shambhala, 1987), pp. 18–19.

8. Richard H. Robinson, *The Buddhist Religion: A Historical Introduction* (Belmont: Dickenson Publishing Co., 1970), pp. 52–53.

9. Ibid., p. 53.

10. Radhakrishnan, *The Hindu View of Life* (New York: The Macmillan Co., 1926), p. 17.

11. Heinrich Zimmer, *Philosophies of India* (Princeton: Princeton University Press, 1951), pp. 79–80.

12. Sarvepalli Radhakrishnan and Charles A. Moore, eds., *A Source Book in Indian Philosophy* (Princeton: Princeton University Press, 1957), p. 38.

13. Ibid., p. 77.

14. Ibid., p. 88.

15. Ibid., p. 89.

16. Radhakrishnan, pp. 24–25.

17. David R. Kinsley, *The Sword and the Flute* (Berkeley: University of California Press, 1975; First Paperback Ed., 1977), p. 2.

18. Susannah Heschel, "Feminism," in *Contemporary Jewish Religious Thought,* eds. Arthur A. Cohen and Paul Mendes-Flohr (New York: Charles Scribner's Sons, 1987), p. 257.

19. Martha A. Ackelsberg, "Spirituality, Community, and Politics: B'not Esh and the Feminist Reconstruction of Judaism," *Journal of Feminist Studies in Religion* (Fall 1986):113.

20. Heschel, p. 257.

21. Sallie McFague, *Metaphorical Theology: Models of God in Religious Language* (Philadelphia: Fortress Press, 1982), p. 2.

22. Ibid., p. 145.

23. Rosemary Radford Ruether, *Sexism and God-Talk: Toward a Feminist Theology* (Boston: Beacon Press, 1983), p. 66.

24. Ibid.

25. Ibid., p. 69.

26. Mary Daly quoted in McFague, p. 147.

27. Ibid.

28. McFague, p. 147.

29. Ursula King, "Goddesses, Witches, Androgyny and Beyond? Feminism and the Transformation of Religious Consciousness," in *Women in the World's Religions: Past and Present,* ed. Ursula King (New York: Paragon House, 1987), p. 212.

30. Ruether, p. 130.

31. Ruether, p. 71.

32. Mary Daly, "After the Death of God the Father: Women's Liberation and

the Transformation of Christian Consciousness," in *Womanspirit Rising,* pp. 57, 59. This article is a reprint from *Commonweal,* March 12, 1971.

33. Merlin Stone, "The Three Faces of Goddess Spirituality," in *The Politics of Women's Spirituality,* ed., Charlene Spretnak (Garden City: Anchor Press, 1982) p. 65.

34. Merlin Stone, "The Great Goddess: Who Was She?" in *The Politics,* p. 8.

35. Carol Christ, *Laughter of Aphrodite* (San Francisco: Harper & Row, 1987), p. 67.

36. Carol Christ, "Why Women Need the Goddess: Phenomenological, Psychological, and Political Reflections," in *Womanspirit Rising,* p. 275.

37. Ibid., p. 277.

38. Christ, *Laughter,* p. 48.

39. Ibid., p. 67.

40. Charlene Spretnak, "Introduction," in *The Politics,* p. xvii.

41. Starhawk, "Witchcraft as Goddess Religion," in *The Politics,* p. 50.

42. Ibid., p. 52.

43. Ibid., p. 54.

44. Ibid.

45. Starhawk, *Truth or Dare: Encounters with Power, Authority, and Mystery* (San Francisco: Harper & Row, 1987), p. 26.

46. Ibid., p. 56.

CHAPTER 5

1. Lana F. Rakow, "Rethinking Gender Research in Communication," *Journal of Communication* 36 (Autumn 1986):23.

2. Barbara Westbrook Eakins and R. Gene Eakins, *Sex Differences in Human Communication* (Boston: Houghton Mifflin Co., 1978), p. 78.

3. Rakow, p. 17.

4. See Cheris Kramarae, *Women and Men Speaking* (Rowley: Newbury House Publishers, Inc., 1981), p. xv.

5. Ibid., p. 156.

6. Ibid., p. 157.

7. Eakins and Eakins, p. 21.

8. See Barrie Thorne, Cheris Kramarae and Nancy Henley, "Language, Gender and Society: Opening a Second Decade of Research," in *Language, Gender, and Society,* eds. Barrie Thorne, Cheris Kramarae, and Nancy Henley (Rowley: Newbury House Publishers, Inc., 1983), p. 8.

9. Eakins and Eakins, p. 181.

10. Kramarae, p. 157.

11. Deborah Borisoff and Lisa Merrill, *The Power to Communicate: Gender Differences as Barriers* (Prospect Heights: Waveland Press, 1985), pp. 12–13.

12. Robin Lakoff, *Language and Woman's Place* (New York: Harper & Row, 1975), p. 11.

13. Ibid.

14. Borisoff and Merrill, p. 10.

15. Specific examples of the male domination of language can be seen in *Webster's Ninth New Collegiate Dictionary's* definitions, which are derogatory to women: e.g.,

master and mistress, bachelor and spinster, and, while the definition of female includes "having some quality (as gentleness or delicacy) associated with the female sex," the definition for male has no such qualities specified.

16. Rakow, p. 17.

17. Eakins and Eakins, p. 114.

18. Wendy Martyna, "Beyond the He/Man Approach: The Case for Nonsexist Language," in *Language, Gender and Society*, p. 34.

19. Ibid.

20. Ibid., p. 30.

21. Thorne, Kramarae, and Henley, p. 10.

22. Eakins and Eakins, p. 140.

23. Ibid., p. 141.

24. Raimundo Panikkar, "The Jordan, the Tiber, and the Ganges," in *The Myth of Christian Uniqueness*, eds. John Hick and Paul F. Knitter (Maryknoll: Orbis Books, 1987), p. 99.

25. Ibid., p. 99.

26. Kramarae, p. 1.

27. Ibid.

28. Ibid., p. xiv.

29. Ibid., p. 4.

30. Ibid.

31. Ibid., p. 5.

32. June O'Connor, "Response to J. Runzo et al.," paper delivered at Blaisdell Conference, Claremont, California in 1987.

CHAPTER 6

1. Paul Knitter, "Toward a Liberation Theology of Religion," in *The Myth of Christian Uniqueness*, p. 179.

2. Ibid., p. 180.

3. Leonard Swidler, "Interreligious and Interideological Dialogue: The Matrix for All Systematic Reflection Today," in *Toward a Universal Theology of Religion*, ed. Leonard Swidler (Maryknoll: Orbis Books, 1987), p. 16.

4. Ibid., p. 17.

5. Knitter, p. 181.

6. Ibid.

7. Mary Ellen Gaylord, "Observations on the Conference," *Journal of Women and Religion* 5 (Summer 1986): pp. 14–15.

8. Diana Eck and Devaki Jain, "Introduction," in *Speaking of Faith: Global Perspectives on Women, Religion and Social Change*, eds. Diana Eck and Devaki Jain (Philadelphia: New Society Publishers, 1987), p. 2.

9. Ibid., p. 1.

10. Ibid., p. 4.

11. Charlotte Bunch, "Beyond Either/Or: Feminist Options," in *Building Feminist Theory: Essays from Quest, a Feminist Quarterly*, ed. The Quest Staff (New York: Longman Inc., 1981), p. 50.

12. Nancy Falk, "Introduction," in *Women, Religion and Social Change*, eds. Yvonne Yazbeck Haddad and Ellison Banks Findly (Albany: State University of New York Press, 1985), p. xv.

13. Mary E. Hunt, "Sharing Feminism: Empowerment or Imperialism?" *Journal of Women in Religion* 1 (Fall 1981):37.

14. Irene Tinker, "Feminist Values: Ethnocentric or Universal?" in *Women in Asia and the Pacific: Towards an East-West Dialogue*, ed. Madeleine J. Goodman (Hawaii: University of Hawaii Press, 1985), p. 117.

15. Transcript of conference, "The Sound of Women's Voices," held at the Claremont Graduate School in Claremont, California on April 16 and 17, 1988.

16. Ibid.

17. Marjorie Suchocki, "Religious Pluralism from a Feminist Perspective," in *The Myth of Christian Uniqueness*, p. 160.

18. Rosalind Delmar, "What is Feminism?" in *What is Feminism?: A Re-examination*, eds. Juliet Mitchell and Ann Oakley (New York: Pantheon Books, 1986), p. 28.

19. Doranne Jacobson, "The Women of North and Central India: Goddesses and Wives," in *Many Sisters: Women in Cross-Cultural Perspective*, ed. Carolyn J. Matthiason (New York: The Free Press, 1974), pp. 136–137.

20. Ibid., p. 134.

21. Valerie J. Hoffman-Ladd, "Polemics on the Modesty and Segregation of Women in Contemporary Egypt," *International Journal of Middle East Studies* 19 (1987):28.

22. Gholam-Reza Vatandoust, "The Status of Iranian Women During the Pahlavi Regime," in *Women and the Family in Iran*, ed. Asghar Fathi (Leiden: E.J. Brill, 1985), p. 124.

23. Hoffman-Ladd., p. 32.

24. Ibid., p. 33.

25. Ibid., p. 40.

26. Alice Appea, Untitled, *Listen to the Women for a Change: A Sixtieth Anniversary Publication of the Women's International League for Peace and Freedom*, ed. Kay Camp (Geneva: Centre International, no date), p. 5.

27. Charlotte Bunch, *Passionate Politics: Feminist Theory in Action* (New York: St. Martin's Press, 1987), p. 328.

28. Ibid., p. 332.

29. Ibid., p. 333.

30. Ibid., p. 334.

31. Ibid., p. 336.

32. Ibid., pp. 329, 331.

33. Tessa Rouverol, "Was It a Blessing?" *Journal of Women and Religion* 5 (Summer 1986):25.

34. Azar Tabari, "The Women's Movement in Iran: A Hopeful Prognosis," *Feminist Studies* 12 (Summer 1986):356–357.

35. Ibid., p. 347.

36. Irena Karska, "Women from all over the World in Dialogue," *Women of the Whole World: Journal of the Women's International Democratic Federation* 3 (1987):2.

37. Ibid., p. 5.

38. *Women in Action* 5 (June 1986).

39. *Women in Action* 6 (December 1986):6.

40. Ibid., p. 7.

41. *Women in Action* 1 (March 1987):24.

42. Ibid.

43. *Women in Action* 2 (June 1987):28.

44. Ibid.

45. Ibid.

46. Jae Hee Kim, Untitled, in *Listen to Women for a Change,* p. 25.

47. Annie Jiagge, Untitled, in *Listen to Women for a Change,* p. 23.

48. Nawaal El Saadawi, "Egypt: When a Woman Rebels..." in *Sisterhood is Global: The International Women's Movement Anthology,* ed. Robin Morgan (Garden City: Anchor Books, 1984), p. 206.

49. Devaki Jain, "INDIA: A Condition Across Caste and Class," in *Sisterhood is Global,* p. 309.

50. Shulamit Aloni, "ISRAEL: Up the Down Escalator," in *Sisterhood is Global,* p. 360.

51. "Statement," *Connexions* 27 (1988), inside cover.

52. Ibid.

53. Ibid., p. 1.

CHAPTER 7

1. Jeanne Audrey Powers, "Women of Faith and This Volume," in *Women of Faith in Dialogue,* ed. Virginia Ramey Mollenkott (New York: Crossroad Publishing Co., 1987), pp. 5–6.

2. "Partners in the Mystery of Redemption: A Pastoral Response to Women's Concerns for Church and Society," *Origins* 17 (April 21, 1988):764.

3. Ibid.

4. Ibid., p. 776.

5. Monika K. Hellwig, "The Critical Function of Feminine Spirituality," *Commonweal* 112 (May 3, 1985):264–68.

6. Deborah Malacky Belonick, "Revelation and Metaphors: The Significance of the Trinitarian Names, Father, Son and Holy Spirit," *Union Seminary Quarterly Review* 40 (1985):34–35.

7. Delores Williams, address given at the School of Theology at Claremont, California on February 9, 1989.

8. Ibid.

9. Kwok Pui Lan, "The Feminist Hermeneutics of Elizabeth Schüssler Fiorenza: An Asian Feminist Response," *East Asia Journal of Theology* 3 (1985):148.

10. Ruether, *Sexism and God-Talk,* p. 138.

11. Ibid., p. 135.

12. Ibid., p. 208.

13. Ibid., p. 209.

14. Mary Daly, "After the Death of God the Father," p. 59.

15. Susannah Heschel, "Feminism," in *Contemporary Jewish Religious Thought,* eds. Arthur A. Cohen and Paul Mendes-Flohr (New York: Charles Scribner's Sons, 1987), p. 258.

16. Blu Greenberg, *On Women and Judaism: A View from Tradition* (Philadelphia: The Jewish Publication Society of America, 1981), p. 5.

17. Ibid.

18. Ibid., p. 11.

19. Ibid., p. 119.

20. Ibid.

21. Ibid., p. 36.

22. Ibid., p. 40.

23. "Modern Women Explain Return to Orthodoxy," *Los Angeles Times*, 7 February 1989, part 5, p. 4.

24. Ibid.

25. Ibid.

26. Susannah Heschel, "Introduction," in *On Being a Jewish Feminist: A Reader*, ed. Susannah Heschel (New York: Schocken Books, 1983), p. xxi.

27. Ibid., p. xxiv.

28. Heschel, "Feminism," p. 258.

29. Drorah Setel, "Roundtable Discussion: Feminist Reflections on Separation and Unity in Jewish Theology," *Journal of Feminist Studies in Religion* (Spring 1986): 114.

30. Ibid., p. 116.

31. Ibid.

32. Ibid.

33. Martha A. Ackelsberg, "Spirituality, Community, and Politics: B'not Esh and the Feminist Reconstruction of Judaism," *Journal of Feminist Studies in Religion* 2 (Fall 1986):111.

34. Ibid., p. 113.

35. Ibid., p. 118.

36. Nadia Hijab, "Nadia Hijab Speaks on Women in the Arab World," *Connexions: An International Women's Quarterly* 28 (1988–1989).

37. Samar F. Masaud, "The Development of Women's Movements in the Muslim World," *Hamdard Islamicus* 8 (Spring 1985):85.

38. Jane I. Smith, "Women in Islam: Equity, and the Search for the Natural Order," *Journal of the American Academy of Religion* 47 (December 1979):517, 528.

39. Jamila Brijbhushan, *Muslim Women: In Purdah and Out of It* (New Delhi: Vikas Publishing House, 1980), p. 61.

40. Ibid., p. 62.

41. Fatima Mernissi, *Beyond the Veil: Male-Female Dynamics in a Modern Muslim Society* (Cambridge: Schenkman Publishing Co., 1975), p. xv.

42. Ibid.

43. Ibid., p. xvi.

44. Miriam Habib, "PAKISTAN: Women—A Fractured Profile," in *Sisterhood is Global*, p. 533.

45. Anita Weiss, "Women's Position in Pakistan: Sociocultural Effects of Islamization," *Asian Survey* 25 (August 1985):872–73.

46. Ibid., p. 873.

47. Ibid.

48. Adele K. Ferdows, "The Status and Rights of Women in Ithna Ashari Shi'i Islam," in *Women and the Family in Iran*, ed. Asghar Fathi (Leiden: E.J. Brill, 1985), p. 34.

49. Yvonne Yazbeck Haddad, "Islam, Women and Revolution in Twentieth-Century Thought," in *Women, Religion and Social Change*, p. 280.

50. Sartaz Aziz and Lawrence Swaim, "Muslim Women Developing a Theory of Islamic Feminism," *Unitarian Universalist World* 16 (August 15, 1985):9.

51. Ibid.

52. Ibid.

53. Ibid., p. 1.

54. Ibid., p. 10.

55. Riffat Hassan, "On Human Rights and the Qur'anic Perspective," *Journal of Ecumenical Studies* 19 (1982):63.

56. Ibid., p. 64.

57. Rita Gross, "Feminism from the Perspective of Buddhist Practice," *Buddhist-Christian Studies* 1 (1981):74.

58. Diana Paul, "Buddhist Attitudes Towards Women's Bodies," *Buddhist-Christian Studies*, 1 (1981):69.

59. Kumiko Uchino, "The Status Elevation Process of Soto Sect Nuns in Modern Japan," in *Speaking of Faith: Cross-cultural Perspectives on Women, Religion and Social Change* (London: The Women's Press, 1986), p. 149.

60. Rita Gross, "Buddhism and Feminism: Toward Their Mutual Transformation, Part II," *The Eastern Buddhist* 19 (Summer 1986):63.

61. Ibid.

62. Eiko Kawamura, "What is it to be Human?: The Zen Perspective on Women's Liberation," a paper discussed in preparation for the conference "The Sound of Women's Voices," Claremont, California, April 16, 17, 1988, p. 4.

63. Ibid.

64. Transcript of Proceedings at Claremont conference.

65. Gross, "Buddhism and Feminism," p. 73.

66. Ellen S. Sidor, "Introduction," in *A Gathering of Spirit: Women Teaching in American Buddhism* (Cumberland: Primary Point Press, 1987), p. 4.

67. Ibid.

68. Jacqueline Schwartz Mandell, "Politics of the Heart," in Sidor, *A Gathering of Spirit*, p. 22.

69. Transcript of conference "The Sound of Women's Voices," Claremont, California, April 16, 17, 1988.

70. Ibid.

71. Katherina von Kellenbach, "Jewish-Christian Dialogue on Feminism and Religion," *Christian Jewish Relations* 19 (1986): 35.

72. Ibid.

73. Ibid., p. 36.

74. A. Roy Eckardt, "Christians, Jews and the Women's Movement," *Christian Jewish Relations* 19 (1986):16.

75. Von Kellenbach, p. 37.

76. Quoted in ibid., p. 36.

77. Susannah Heschel, "Current Issues in Jewish Feminist Theology," *Christian Jewish Relations* 19 (1986):23.

78. Ibid., p. 28.

79. Mindy Avra Portnoy, "Prelude to Dialogue: What Christians Need to Know About Jews." *NICM Journal* 8 (Spring–Summer 1983):77.

80. Ibid.

81. Katherine K. Young, "Hinduism," in *Women in World Religions*, ed. Arvind Sharma (Albany: State University of New York Press, 1987), p. 87.

82. Transcript of Conference at Claremont, California, April 16, 17, 1988.

83. Ibid.

84. Ibid.

85. Ibid.
86. Ibid.

CHAPTER 8

1. Nelle Morton, *The Journey Is Home* (Boston: Beacon Press, 1985), p. 55.
2. Ibid.
3. Culpepper, "Philosophia," (dissertation).
4. Culpepper, "Philosophia: Feminist Methodology for Constructing a Female Train of Thought," *Journal of Feminist Studies in Religion* 3 (1987):15.
5. John Hick, *Problems of Religious Pluralism* (New York: St. Martin's Press, 1985), p. 39.
6. Ibid.
7. Ibid.
8. Gerard Loughlin, "Noumenon and Phenomena," *Religious Studies* 23 (December 1987):497.
9. Ibid.
10. Diana Eck and Devaki Jain, "Introduction," in *Speaking of Faith: Global Perspectives on Women, Religion and Social Change,* eds. Diana Eck and Devaki Jain (Philadelphia: New Society Publishers, 1987), p. 12.
11. Culpepper, *Journal of Feminist Studies*, pp. 9–10.
12. Culpepper, dissertation, p. 225.
13. Ibid., pp. 226–27.
14. Sarah Cunningham, "A Meeting of the Minds," in *Women of Faith in Dialogue*, p. 16.

CHAPTER 9

1. Riffat Hassan, "Dialogue From Below," *Religion and Intellectual Life* 4 (Summer 1987):48.
2. Eakins and Eakins, p. 49.
3. This suggestion was discussed with Beverly Harrison of Union Theological Seminary in New York at the American Academy of Religion Conference in Chicago in November, 1988. Her agreement with the observation confirmed the possibility of its truth.
4. Paul Knitter, "Confirmation Through Conflict? Some Questions for the Dialogue of Touchstones," *Horizons* 14 (Spring 1987):109.
5. Ibid., p. 110.
6. Maurice Friedman, "Conflict in the Dialogue of Touchstones: Reply to Paul F. Knitter," *Horizons* 14 (Spring 1987):111.
7. Ibid., p. 112.
8. Ibid., p. 113.
9. Eck and Jain, pp. 13–14, 15.
10. David Tracy, "Christianity in the Wider Context: Demands and Transformations," *Religion and Intellectual Life* 4 (Summer 1987):19.

CONCLUSION

1. Harvey Cox, *Many Mansions: A Christian's Encounter With Other Faiths* (Boston: Beacon Press, 1988), pp. 57–58.

2. Robin Morgan, "Introduction," *Sisterhood Is Powerful: An Anthology of Writings From the Women's Liberation Movement* (New York: Random House, 1970), pp. xv–xvi.

3. Carol Christ, *Laughter of Aphrodite: Reflections on a Journey to the Goddess* (San Francisco: Harper & Row, 1987), p. xiv.

4. Welch, pp. 85–86.

5. Eck and Jain, p. 247.

6. Mollenkott, p. 6.

7. Borrowed from Adrienne Rich's title, *A Wild Patience Has Taken Me This Far.*

8. David Lochhead, *The Dialogical Imperative: A Christian Reflection in Interfaith Encounter* (Maryknoll: Orbis Books, 1988), pp. 79–80.

9. Hick, *Problems of Religious Pluralism*, p. 30.

10. Gordon D. Kaufman, "Religious Diversity, Historical Consciousness, and Christian Theology," in *The Myth of Christian Uniqueness*, p. 3.

11. Swidler, p. 16.

12. Ibid., p. 17.

13. Lochhead, p. 75.

14. Ursula King, in *Women in the World's Religions,* p. 216.

Bibliography

Ackelsberg, Martha A."Spirituality, Community, and Politics: B'not Esh and the Feminist Reconstruction of Judaism." *Journal of Feminist Studies in Religion* (Fall 1986): 109–120.

Aloni, Shulamit. "ISRAEL: Up the Down Escalator." In *Sisterhood is Global: The International Women's Movement Anthology*, pp. 360–63. Edited by Robin Morgan. Garden City: Anchor Books, 1984.

Appea, Alice. Untitled. In *Listen to the Women: A Sixtieth Anniversary Publication of the Women's International League for Peace and Freedom*, p. 5. Edited by Kay Camp. Geneva: Centre International, no date.

Aquino, Belinda. "Feminism Across Cultures." In *Women in Asia and the Pacific: Towards an East-West Dialogue*. pp. 317–51. Edited by Madeleine J. Goodman. Hawaii: University of Hawaii Press, 1985.

Aziz, Sartaz. "Recollections of a Muslim Woman." *Women of Power* 4 (Fall 1986): 53–55.

———. and Swaim, Lawrence. "Muslim Women Developing a Theory of Islamic Feminism." *Unitarian Universalist World* 16 (August 15, 1985): 10–11.

Belonick, Deborah Malacky. "Revelation and Metaphors: The Significance of the Trinitarian Names, Father, Son and Holy Spirit." *Union Seminary Quarterly Review* 40 (1985): 31–42.

Blum, Lawrence A. "Kant's and Hegel's Moral Rationalism: A Feminist Perspective." *Canadian Journal of Philosophy* 12 (June 1982): 287–303.

Borisoff, Deborah and Merrill, Lisa. *The Power to Communicate: Gender Differences as Barriers*. Prospect Heights: Waveland Press, 1985.

Bourque, Susan C. and Divine, Donna Robinson. *Women Living Change*. Philadelphia: Temple University Press, 1985.

Braidotti, Rosi. "Ethics Revisited: Women and/in Philosophy." In *Feminist Challenges: Social and Political Theory*, pp. 44–60. Edited by Carole Pateman and Elizabeth Gross. Boston: Northeastern University Press, 1986.

Brijbhushan, Jamila. *Muslim Women: In Purdah and Out of It*. New Delhi: Vikas Publishing House, 1980.

Brown, Penelope and Jordanova, L. "Oppressive Dichotomies: The Nature/Culture Debate." In *The Changing Woman*, pp. 389–99. Edited by Elizabeth Whitelegg, Madeleine Arnot, et al. Oxford: Martin Robertson, 1982.

Bunch, Charlotte. "Beyond Either/Or: Feminist Options." In *Building Feminist Theory: Essays from Quest, A Feminist Quarterly*, pp. 44–56. Edited by The Quest Staff. New York: Longman Inc., 1981.

———. *Passionate Politics: Feminist Theory in Action*. New York: St. Martin's Press, 1987.

Carmody, Denise Lardner and Carmody, John Tully. *Ways to the Center*. 2nd ed. Belmont: Wadsworth Publishing Co., 1984.

Chandran, J. R. "Plurality of Religious Faith and Living in Community." *Religion and Society* 33 (September 1986): 71–80.

Chatterji, Jyotsna. "Editorial: Religions and the Status of Women." *Religion and Society: Quarterly Bulletin of The Christian Institute for the Study of Religion and Society* 32 (June 1985): 1–2.

Christ, Carol P. *Laughter of Aphrodite: Reflections on a Journey to the Goddess.* San Francisco: Harper & Row, 1987.

————. "Why Women Need the Goddess: Phenomenological, Psychological, and Political Reflections." In *Womanspirit Rising*, pp. 273–87. Edited by Carol P. Christ and Judith Plaskow. New York: Harper & Row, 1979.

Code, Lorraine. "Experience, Knowledge, and Responsibility." In *Feminist Perspectives in Philosophy*, pp. 187–204. Edited by Morwenna Griffiths and Margaret Whitford. Bloomington: Indiana University Press, 1988.

Connexions: An International Women's Quarterly 27 (1988).

Cooey, Paula. "The Power of Transformation and the Transformation of Power." *Journal of Feminist Studies in Religion* 1 (Spring 1985): 23–36.

Culpepper, Emily Erwin. "Philosophia: Feminist Methodology for Constructing a Female Train of Thought." *Journal of Feminist Studies in Religion* 3 (Fall 1987): 7–16.

————. "Philosophia in a Feminist Key: Revolt of the Symbols." Ph.D. dissertation, Harvard University, 1983.

Cunningham, Sarah. "A Meeting of the Minds." In *Women of Faith in Dialogue*, pp. 9–16. Edited by Virginia Ramey Mollenkott. New York: Crossroad, 1987.

Daly, Mary. "After the Death of God the Father: Women's Liberation and the Transformation of Christian Consciousness." In *Womanspirit Rising*, pp. 53–62. Edited by Carol P. Christ and Judith Plaskow. New York: Harper & Row, 1979.

————. *Pure Lust: Elemental Feminist Philosophy.* Boston: Beacon Press, 1984.

Delmar, Rosalind. "What is Feminism?" In *What is Feminism? A Reexamination*, pp. 2–33. Edited by Juliet Mitchell and Ann Oakley. New York: Pantheon Books, 1986.

Dunfee, Susan Nelson. "The Sin of Hiding: A Feminist Critique of Reinhold Niebuhr's Account of the Sin of Pride." *Soundings* 65 (Fall 1982): 316–27.

Eakins, Barbara Westbrook and Eakins, R. Gene. *Sex Differences in Human Communication.* Boston: Houghton Mifflin Co., 1978.

Eck, Diana and Jain, Devaki. "Introduction: Women, Religion and Social Change." In *Speaking of Faith: Global Perspectives on Women, Religion and Social Change*, pp. 1–15. Edited by Diana Eck and Devaki Jain. Philadelphia: New Society Publishers, 1987.

Eckardt, A. Roy. "Christians, Jews and the Women's Movement." *Christian Jewish Relations* 19 (1986): 13–22.

El Saadawi, Nawal. "EGYPT: When a Woman Rebels." In *Sisterhood is Global: The International Women's Movement Anthology*, pp. 199–206. Edited by Robin Morgan. Garden City: Anchor Books, 1984.

Falk, Nancy. "Introduction." In *Women, Religion and Social Change*, pp. xv–xxi. Edited by Yvonne Yazbeck Haddad and Ellison Banks Findly. Albany: State University of New York Press, 1985.

Ferdows, Adele K. "The Status and Rights of Women in Ithna Ashari Shi'i Islam." In *Women and the Family in Iran*, pp. 13–36. Edited by Asghar Fathi. Leiden: E. J. Brill, 1985.

Friedman, Lenore, ed. *Meetings With Remarkable Women: Buddhist Teachers in America*. Boston: Shambhala, 1987.

Friedman, Maurice. "Conflict in the Dialogue of Touchstones: Reply to Paul F. Knitter." *Horizons* 14 (Spring 1987): 111–14.

———. "The Dialogue of Touchstones: An Approach to Interreligious Dialogue." *Horizons* 14 (Spring 1987): 97–107.

Gardiner, Linda. "Can This Discipline Be Saved? Feminist Theory Challenges Mainstream Philosophy." Working Paper #118. Wellesley College Center for Research on Women, 1983.

Gaylord, Mary Ellen. "Observations on the Conference." *Journal of Women and Religion* 5 (Summer 1986): 12–15.

Ghotoskar, Sujata and Kanhere, Vijay. "The Role of Women in Social Change and People's Movements." *Social Action* 34 (April–June 1984): 132–36.

Glennon, Lynda M. *Women and Dualism: A Sociology of Knowledge Analysis*. New York: Longman, 1979.

Greenberg, Blu. *On Women and Judaism: A View from Tradition*. Philadelphia: The Jewish Publication Society of America, 1981.

Grimshaw, Jean. *Philosophy and Feminist Thinking*. Minneapolis: University of Minnesota Press, 1986.

Gross, Elizabeth. "Conclusion: What is Feminist Theory." In *Feminist Challenges: Social and Political Theory*, pp. 190–204. Edited by Carol Pateman and Elizabeth Gross. Boston: Northeastern University Press, 1986.

Gross, Rita. "Buddhism and Feminism: Toward Their Mutual Transformation, Part II." *The Eastern Buddhist* 19 (Summer 1986): 62–74.

———. "Feminism from the Perspective of Buddhist Practice." *Buddhist-Christian Studies* 1 (1981): 73–82.

Habib, Miriam. "PAKISTAN: Women—A Fractured Profile." In *Sisterhood is Global: The International Women's Movement Anthology*, pp. 530–35. Edited by Robin Morgan. Garden City: Anchor Books, 1984.

Haddad, Yvonne Yazbeck. "Islam, Women and Revolution in Twentieth-Century Thought." In *Women, Religion and Social Change*, pp. 275–306. Edited by Yvonne Yazbeck Haddad and Ellison Banks Findly. Albany: State University of New York Press, 1985.

Harding, Sandra. "Is Gender a Variable in Conceptions of Rationality? A Survey of Issues." In *Beyond Domination: New Perspectives on Women and Philosophy*, pp. 43–63. Edited by Carol Gould. Totowa: Rowman and Allanheld, 1983.

———. *The Science Question in Feminism*. Ithaca: Cornell University Press, 1986.

———. and Hintikka, Merrill B., eds. *Discovering Reality: Feminist Perspectives on Epistemology, Metaphysics, Methodology, and Philosophy of Science*. Boston: D. Reidel Pub. Co., 1983.

Hartsock, Nancy. "Political Change: Two Perspectives on Power." In *Building Feminist Theory: Essays from the QUEST, a Feminist Quarterly*, pp. 3–19. New York: Longman Inc., 1981.

Hassan, Riffat. "Dialogue From Below." *Religion and Intellectual Life* 4 (Summer 1987): 47–49.

———. "On Human Rights and the Qur'anic Perspective." *Journal of Ecumenical Studies* 19 (1982): 51–65.

———. "Messianism and Islam." *Journal of Ecumenical Studies* 22 (Spring 1985): 261–91.

Hellwig, Monika K. "The Critical Function of Feminine Spirituality." *Commonweal* 112 (May 3, 1985) : 264–58.

Heschel, Susannah. "Current Issues in Jewish Feminist Theology." *Christian Jewish Relations* 19 (1986): 23–32.

———. "Feminism." In *Contemporary Jewish Religious Thought*, pp. 255–59. Edited by Arthur A. Cohen and Paul Mendes-Flohr. New York: Charles Scribner's Sons, 1987.

———, ed. *On Being a Jewish Feminist: A Reader*. New York: Schocken Books, 1983.

Hick, John. *An Interpretation of Religion*. New Haven: Yale University Press, 1989.

———. "On Grading Religions." *Religious Studies* 17 (December, 1981): 451–67.

———. "The Non-Absoluteness of Christianity." In *The Myth of Christian Uniqueness: Toward a Pluralistic Theology of Religions*, pp. 16–36. Edited by Paul Knitter and John Hick. Maryknoll: Orbis Books, 1987.

———. *Problems of Religious Pluralism*. New York: St. Martin's Press, 1985.

Hijab, Nadia. "Nadia Hijab Speaks on Women in the Arab World." *Connexions: An International Women's Quarterly* 28 (1988–89): 2–3.

Hoffman-Ladd, Valerie J. "Polemics on the Modesty and Segregation of Women in Contemporary Egypt." *International Journal of Middle East Studies* 19 (1987): 23–50.

Hunt, Mary E. "Sharing Feminism: Empowerment or Imperialism?" *Journal of Women in Religion* 1 (Fall 1981): 33–46.

Jacobson, Doranne. "The Women of North and Central India: Goddesses and Wives." In *Many Sisters: Women in Cross-Cultural Perspective*, pp. 99–175. Edited by Carolyn J. Matthiason. New York: The Free Press, 1974.

Jaggar, Alison M. "Human Biology in Feminist Theory: Sexual Equality Reconsidered." In *Beyond Domination: New Perspectives on Women and Philosophy*, pp. 31–42. Edited by Carol C. Gould. Totowa: Rowan and Allanheld, 1983.

Jain, Devaki. "INDIA: A Condition Across Caste and Class." In *Sisterhood is Global: The International Women's Movement Anthology*, pp. 305–309. Edited by Robin Morgan. Garden City: Anchor Books, 1984.

Jiagge, Annie. In *Listen to Women for a Change: A Sixtieth Anniversary Publication of the Women's International League for Peace and Freedom*, p. 23. Edited by Kay Camp. Geneva: Centre International, no date.

Jung, L. Shannon. "Feminism and Spatiality: Ethics and the Recovery of a Hidden Dimension." *Journal of Feminist Studies in Religion* 4 (Spring 1988): 55–71.

Kant, Immanuel. "Foundations of the Metaphysics of Morals." In *Kant: Selections*, pp. 244–98. Edited by Lewis White Beck. New York: Macmillan Publishing Co., 1988.

Karska, Irena. "Women All Over the World in Dialogue." *Women of the Whole World: Journal of the Women's International Democratic Federation* 3 (1987): 1–5.

Kawamura, Eiko. "What is it to be Human?: The Zen Perspective on Women's Liberation." Paper written in preparation for conference in Claremont, California, April 16–17, 1988.

Keller, Evelyn Fox. "Gender and Science." In *Twenty Questions: An Introduction to Philosophy*. Edited by G. Lee Bowie, Meredith W. Michaels, and Robert C. Solomon. San Diego: Harcourt Brace Jovanovich, 1988.

Kim, Jae Hee. In *Listen to Women for a Change: A Sixtieth Anniversary Publication of the Women's International League for Peace and Freedom*, p. 25. Edited by Kay Camp. Geneva: Centre International, no date.

King, Ursula. "Goddesses, Witches, Androgyny and Beyond? Feminism and the Transformation of Religious Consciousness." In *Women in the World's Religions*, pp. 201–18. Edited by Ursula King. New York: Paragon House, 1987.

Kinsley, David R. *The Sword and the Flute*. Berkeley: University of California Press, 1975; paperback edition, 1977.

Knitter, Paul. "Confirmation Through Conflict? Some Questions for the Dialogue of Touchstones." *Horizons* 14 (Spring 1987): 108–110.

――――. "Toward a Liberation Theology of Religions." In *The Myth of Christian Uniqueness: Toward a Pluralistic Theology of Religions*, pp. 178–200. Edited by John Hick and Paul F. Knitter. Maryknoll: Orbis Books, 1987.

Kramarae, Cheris. *Women and Men Speaking*. Rowley: Newbury House Publishers, Inc., 1981.

Lakoff, Robin. *Language and Woman's Place*. New York: Harper & Row, 1975.

Lloyd, Genevieve. *The Man of Reason: 'Male' and 'Female' in Western Philosophy*. London: Methuen and Co., 1984.

Loughlin, Gerard. "Noumenon and Phenomena." *Religious Studies* 23 (December 1987): 493–508.

Lowe, Marian. "The Dialectic of Biology and Culture." In *Women's Nature: Rationalizations of Inequality*, pp. 39–62. Edited by Marian Lowe and Ruth Hubbard. New York: Pergamon Press, 1983.

Mandell, Jacqueline Schwartz. "Politics of the Heart." In *A Gathering of Spirit*, pp. 23–25. Edited by Ellen S. Sidor. Cumberland: Primary Point Press, 1985.

Marshall, Susan E. "Paradoxes of Change: Culture Crises, Islamic Revival, and the Reactivation of Patriarchy." *Journal of Asian and African Studies* 19 (January and April 1984): 1–17.

Martyna, Wendy. "Beyond the He/Man Approach: The Case for Nonsexist Language." In *Language, Gender and Society*, pp. 25–37. Edited by Barrie Thorne, Cheris Kramarae, and Nancy Henley. Rowley: Newbury House, 1983.

Masaud, Samar F. "The Development of Women's Movements in the Muslim World." *Hamdard Islamicus* 8 (Spring 1985): 81–86.

Matthiasson, Carolyn J. "Introduction." In *Many Sisters: Women in Cross-Cultural Perspective*, pp. xv–xxi. Edited by Carolyn J. Mathiasson. New York: The Free Press, 1974.

McFague, Sallie. *Metaphorical Theology: Models of God in Religious Language*. Philadelphia: Fortress Press, 1985.

McMillan, Carol. *Women, Reason and Nature: Some Philosophical Problems with Feminism*. Princeton: Princeton University Press, 1982.

Mernissi, Fatima. *Beyond the Veil: Male-Female Dynamics in a Modern Muslim Society*. Cambridge: Schenkman Publishing Co., 1975.

Miller, Jean Baker. *Toward a New Psychology of Women*. 2nd ed. Boston: Beacon Press, 1986.

Morgan, Robin. "Introduction." *Sisterhood is Powerful: An Anthology of Writings From the Women's Liberation Movement*, pp. xii–xviii. New York: Random House, 1970.

Panikkar, Raimundo. *The Unknown Christ of Hinduism*. Revised Edition. Maryknoll: Orbis Books, 1981.

"Partners in the Mystery of Redemption: A Pastoral Response to Women's Concerns for Church and Society." *Origins: NC Documentary Service* 17 (April 21, 1988): 757–88.

Paul, Diana. "Buddhist Attitudes Toward Women's Bodies." *Buddhist-Christian Studies* 1 (1981): 63–71.

Pearsall, Marilyn, ed. *Women and Values: Readings in Recent Feminist Philosophy.* Belmont: Wadsworth Publishing Co., 1986.

Portnoy, Mindy Avra. "Prelude to Dialogue: What Christians Need to Know About Jews." *NICM Journal* 8 (Spring–Summer 1983): 73–83.

Powers, Jeanne Audrey. "Women of Faith and This Volume." In *Women of Faith in Dialogue*, pp. 3–6. Edited by Virginia Ramey Mollenkott. New York: Crossroad Publishing Co., 1987.

Pui Lan, Kwok. "The Feminist Hermeneutics of Elizabeth Schüssler Fiorenza: An Asian Feminist Response." *East Asia Journal of Theology* 3 (1985): 147–53.

Radhakrishnan. *The Hindu View of Life.* New York: The Macmillan Co., 1926.

Radhakrishnan, Sarvepalli and Moore, Charles A., eds. *A Sourcebook in Indian Philosophy.* Princeton: Princeton University Press, 1957.

Rakow, Lana F. "Rethinking Gender Research in Communication." *Journal of Communication* 36 (Autumn 1986): 11–26.

Robb, Carol S. "A Framework for Feminist Ethics." In *Women's Consciousness, Women's Conscience: A Reader in Feminist Ethics*, pp. 211–33. Edited by Barbara Hilkert Andolsen, Christine E. Gudorf and Mary D. Pellauer. San Francisco: Harper & Row, 1985.

Robinson, Richard H. *The Buddhist Religion: A Historical Introduction.* Belmont: Dickenson Publishing Co., 1970.

Rouverol, Tessa. "Was It a Blessing?" *Journal of Women and Religion* 5 (Summer 1986): 23–27.

Ruether, Rosemary Radford. *Sexism and God-Talk: Toward a Feminist Theology.* Boston: Beacon Press, 1983.

Ruth, Sheila. "Methodocracy, Misogyny, and Bad Faith: The Response of Philosophy." In *Men's Studies Modified*, pp. 43–53. Edited by Dale Spender. Oxford: Pergamon Press, 1981.

Schmidt, Roger. *Exploring Religion.* 2nd ed. Belmont: Wadsworth Publishing Co., 1988.

Seller, Anne. "Realism versus Relativism: Towards a Politically Adequate Epistemology." In *Feminist Perspectives in Philosophy*, pp. 169–86. Edited by Morwenna Griffiths and Margaret Whitford. Bloomington: Indiana University Press, 1988.

Setel, T. Drorah. "Roundtable Discussion: Feminist Reflections on Separation and Unity in Jewish Theology." *Journal of Feminist Studies in Religion* (Spring 1986): 113–18.

Sidor, Ellen S. "Introduction." In *A Gathering of Spirit: Women Teaching in American Buddhism*, pp. 2–4. Edited by Ellen S. Sidor. Cumberland: Primary Point Press, 1987.

Smith, Jane I. "Women in Islam: Equity, Equality, and the Search for the Natural Order." *Journal of the American Academy of Religion* 47 (December 1979): 517–37.

Smith, Ruth L. "Feminism and the Moral Subject." In *Women's Consciousness, Women's Conscience: A Reader in Feminist Ethics*, pp. 235–50. Edited by Barbara Hilkert Andolsen, Christine E. Gudorf and Mary D. Pellauer. San Francisco: Harper & Row, 1985.

Smith, Wilfred Cantwell. *Towards a World Theology.* Philadelphia: The Westminster Press, 1981.

Spender, Dale. *For the Record: The Making and Meaning of Feminist Knowledge.* London: The Women's Press, 1985.

Spretnak, Charlene. "Introduction." In *The Politics of Women's Spirituality*, pp. xi–xxx. Edited by Charlene Spretnak. Garden City: Anchor Press, 1982.

Starhawk. "Witchcraft as Goddess Religion." In *The Politics of Women's Spirituality*, pp. 49–56. Edited by Charlene Spretnak. Garden City: Anchor Press, 1982.

Stone, Merlin. "The Great Goddess: Who Was She?" In *The Politics of Women's Spirituality*, pp. 7–21. Edited by Charlene Spretnak. Garden City: Anchor Press, 1982.

————. "The Three Faces of Goddess Spirituality." In *The Politics of Women's Spirituality*, pp. 64–70. Edited by Charlene Spretnak. Garden City: Anchor Press, 1982.

Swidler, Leonard. "Interreligious and Interideological Dialogue: The Matrix for All Systematic Reflection Today." In *Toward a Universal Theology of Religion*, pp. 5–50. Edited by Leonard Swidler. Maryknoll: Orbis Books, 1988.

Tabari, Azar. "The Women's Movement In Iran: A Hopeful Prognosis." *Feminist Studies* 12 (Summer 1986): 343–60.

Thorne, Barrie; Kramarae, Cheris and Henley, Nancy. eds. *Language, Gender and Society.* Rowley: Newbury House Publishers, Inc., 1983.

Tinker, Irene. "Feminist Values: Ethnocentric or Universal?" In *Women in Asia and the Pacific: Towards an East-West Dialogue*, pp. 103–25. Edited by Madeleine J. Goodman. Hawaii: University of Hawaii Press, 1985.

Tracy, David. "Christianity in the Wider Context: Demands and Transformations." *Religion and Intellectual Life* 4 (Summer 1987): 7–20.

Tuana, Nancy. "A Reply to Laura Purdy." *Hypatia: A Journal of Feminist Philosophy* 1 (Spring 1986): 175–78.

Uchino, Kumiko. "The Status Elevation Process of Soto Sect Nuns in Modern Japan." In *Speaking of Faith: Cross-cultural Perspectives on Women, Religion and Social Change*, pp. 159–73. Edited by Diana Eck and Devaki Jain. London: The Women's Press, 1986.

Vatandoust, Gholam-Reza. "The Status of Iranian Women During the Pahlavi Regime." In *Women and the Family in Iran*, pp. 107–30. Edited by Asghar Fathi. Leiden: E.J. Brill, 1985.

Von Kellenbach, Katherina. "Jewish-Christian Dialogue on Feminism and Religion." *Christian Jewish Relations* 19 (1986): 33–40.

Weiss, Anita M. "Women's Position in Pakistan: Sociocultural Effects of Islamization." *Asian Survey* 25 (August 1985): 863–80.

Welch, Sharon D. *Communities of Resistance and Solidarity: A Feminist Theology of Liberation.* Maryknoll: Orbis Books, 1985.

Whitbeck, Caroline. "A Different Reality: Feminist Ontology." In *Beyond Domination: New Perspectives on Women and Philosophy*, pp. 64–88. Edited by Carol Gould. Totowa: Rowman & Allanheld, 1983.

Women in Action 5 (June 1986): 26.

———— 6 (December 1986): 6.

———— 1 (March 1987): 24.

———— 2 (June, 1987): 28–29.

Young, Katherine K., "Hinduism." In *Women in World Religions*, pp. 59–103. Edited by Arvind Sharma. Albany: State University of New York Press, 1987.

Zimmer, Heinrich. *Philosophies of India*. Princeton: Princeton University Press, 1951.

Zweig, Arnulf, ed. In *Kant: Philosophical Correspondence 1759–99*. Chicago: University of Chicago Press, 1967.

Index

BENNY BREAKIRON

IN

THE TWELVE TRIALS OF BENNY BREAKIRON

SCENARIO: YVAN DELPORTE AND *Peyo*

DRAWINGS: *Peyo* AND *Walthéry*

PAPERCUTZ™

NEW YORK

Peyo GRAPHIC NOVELS AVAILABLE FROM **PAPERCUTZ** ™

BENNY BREAKIRON

1. THE RED TAXIS
2. MADAME ADOLPHINE
3. TWELVE TRIALS OF BENNY BREAKIRON
4. UNCLE PLACID (COMING SOON)

THE SMURFS

1. THE PURPLE SMURFS
2. THE SMURFS AND THE MAGIC FLUTE
3. THE SMURF KING
4. THE SMURFETTE
5. THE SMURFS AND THE EGG
6. THE SMURFS AND THE HOWLIBIRD
7. THE ASTROSMURF
8. THE SMURF APPRENTICE
9. GARGAMEL AND THE SMURFS
10. THE RETURN OF THE SMURFETTE
11. THE SMURF OLYMPICS
12. SMURF VS. SMURF
13. SMURF SOUP
14. THE BABY SMURF
15. THE SMURFLINGS
15. THE AEROSMURF

BENNY BREAKIRON graphic novels are available in hardcover only for $11.99 each. THE SMURFS graphic novels are available in paperback for $5.99 each and in hardcover for $10.99 each at booksellers everywhere. You can also order online at www.papercutz.com. Or call 1-800-886-1223, Monday through Friday, 9 – 5 EST. MC, Visa, and AmEx accepted. To order by mail, please add $4.00 for postage and handling for first book ordered, $1.00 for each additional book and make check payable to NBM Publishing. Send to: Papercutz, 160 Broadway, Suite 700, East Wing, New York, NY 10038.

BENNY BREAKIRON and THE SMURFS graphic novels are also available digitally wherever e-books are sold.

WWW.PAPERCUTZ.COM

BENNY BREAKIRON
#3 "The Twelve Trials
of Benny Breakiron"

© Peyo - 2014 - Licensed through Lafig Belgium - www.smurf.com

English Translation Copyright © 2014 by Papercutz.
All rights reserved.

Joe Johnson, TRANSLATION
Adam Grano, DESIGN AND PRODUCTION
Janice Chiang, LETTERING
Matt. Murray, SMURF CONSULTANT
Beth Scorzato, PRODUCTION COORDINATOR
Michael Petranek, ASSOCIATE EDITOR
Jim Salicrup
EDITOR-IN-CHIEF

ISBN: 978-1-59707-492-6

Papercutz books may be purchased for business or promotional use. For information on bulk purchases please contact Macmillan Corporate and Premium Sales Department at (800) 221-7945 x5442.

PRINTED IN CHINA JANUARY 2014 BY NEW ERA PRINTING LTD.
UNIT C, 8F, WORLDWIDE CENTRE
123 TUNG CHAU STREET, HONG KONG

DISTRIBUTED BY MACMILLAN
FIRST PAPERCUTZ PRINTING

THE TWELVE TRIALS
OF BENNY BREAKIRON

Every year, Vivejoie-la-Grande's giant fair attracts a large crowd from all corners...

Benny Breakiron, like every boy his age, is crazy about fairs...

Step right up, ladies and gents! Come see Samson, the strongest man in the world, who's going to effortlessly break this heavy, steel chain!

~Humph!~

GO AHEAD, BUDDY!

HA!

And voilà!... And that's not all! But first, I'll pass my hat around to encourage the artist! Thank you, ladies and gents!

He's so strong!

Hey, monsieur, what do you do when you have a cold?

?

4

Monsieur Dussiflard!

Aren't you ashamed of attacking someone smaller than you, you big bully? What did he do to you?

He's demolished my machine! So what will I do now? Huh?

What? You dare accuse a little boy like Benny of breaking your machine?... Why, you're crazy!

And don't let me catch you again, because I'll send the police, I will! I never...!

Hey, Monsieur Dussiflard, he was right. I'm the one who broke his machine!

No way!

Yes! Don't tell anyone, but I'm very, very strong!

Sure you are, Benny, sure you are! Okay, come on, we'll buy some pommes frites! (1)

DUSSIFLARD! What a lucky break! I was looking everywhere for you!

TOASTIES

Verchaval! Old Vercheval! What's become of you? Still a reporter?

Yes! And you? Are you still driving taxis?

Old friend, I have extraordinary news for you! Come have a drink. I'll explain!

It's an unheard of, fantastic, incredible story!

Come, Benny!

Okay! Sit down! Do you remember the emir?

Hidienn ed Ghrinouitch? Of course! What's he been up to these thirty years?

He returned to his country... I'm back from doing a story there... Brace yourself: we're all going to become **BILLIONAIRES!**

(1) Pommes frites = French fries.

5

Bi-- Billionaires! Is this a joke? How--?

No, old friend! Our land! A company has discovered the richest oil deposit in the world there!

That's incredible!

Exactly! You still have your piece of paper, I hope?

Of course-- it's at home!... Billionaires! I wasn't expecting that!

Okay, listen, I have to get going! I have an important meeting! No, forget it, it's on me!...

I'll come by your place tonight around eight! We'll be able to discuss all this more comfortably! Do you still live on Big Pump street?

Yes!...

Good, see you tonight!

A billionaire!...

What's all this about land, Monsieur Dussiflard?

Ha! Ha! It's a mighty old story, Benny! Here, look at this photo!

Oh! Why that's you! And isn't that the man who just left?

Yes! With old Vercheval and some other friends, we used to have the Vivejoie Jazz Band...

"...We'd play at dances, on Sundays, and that'd make us a little pocket money!

"One day, a young Middle Eastern man came in! It was Hidienn ed Ghrinouitch."

6

Hidienn, who'd come to do his studies in Europe, really liked our music! He'd come to each of our dances!

"One evening, he'd offered a round to the entire room! But when it came time to pay, he realized he had no money! The bar owner threatened our friend with prison!"

"So, to help him out, we all chipped in! And since the amount wasn't sufficient, we proposed to the owner to come play a few Sundays for free!"

"To show us his gratitude, the young man offered to us the deed to a fiefdom in his country!

Oh! It's nothing much! A hundred or so square miles of sand, but it belongs to me personally!

"But the question arose: who was going to safeguard the deed?"

Let's tear it into nine pieces! It won't have any value unless it's complete!

RRIPP

Shortly after, Hidienn returned to his country to succeed his father, the emir! And now it seems they've found oil on our land!

But then it's true you're a billionaire?

Yes indeed, Benny! Come, we have to celebrate this! I'll pay for all the attractions in the fair for you!

Goodness! Seven-thirty already! And Vercheval's coming at eight! We must get home!

Will you show me your piece of paper?

Yes! Come in!

That's strange. I'm sure I shut my door when I left!

5.

7

Why-- my house has been burglarized!

My savings!

It can't be--! It's still here! It's incomprehensible!

And your piece of paper that makes you a billionaire?

It's in my keepsake chest upstairs in the attic!

Here it is! Anyhow, nobody knows the value of this piece of paper, so the burglars wouldn't have ever taken it!

But what were they looking for then?

I don't know! I-- Hey! The telephone!

DRIIIING

Hello?

Good evening, sir! I'm Mister Vercheval's secretary! He told me to tell you he wouldn't be able to meet at your home this evening, but he asks for you to meet him as soon as possible at 27 Greenwood Street!

Ah! I was forgetting! He said you should bring your paper with you!

Okay! Thank you, Miss!

Vercheval can't come! I must join him elsewhere with my paper!

I'll go with you, Monsieur Dussiflard!

No, Benny! It's late! You go on home!

BANDITS! Give me Monsieur Dussiflard's paper!

A kid! Where'd he come from?

Don't worry! I'll take care of him!

Don't hurt him too much, Joe! After all, he's just a kid!

POW

Joe! What happened to you? Answer me!...

For the last time, give me that paper!

Now you're making me mad! You're gonna get a—

POW

I'll need a rope to tie them up! But where can I find one?

Too bad! Make do with what you have, like the schoolteacher says!

GROING

Oh! My head!... Benny! What are you doing here? What happened?

They're bandits, Monsieur Dussiflard! They tried to take your piece of paper!

Who paid you to do your dirty work?

We don't know! It was some guy with glasses and a mustache! I think he was a reporter!

VERCHEVAL!

Vercheval! The bandit! He wants to keep the land the emir gave us all for himself!

But then, we must warn the others who have a piece of paper like you!

You're right, Benny! Alas! The only one whose address I have is Lorgelet, who played the saxophone!

He became a bank director in the middle of the country! It's too late to call him, but if we leave now, we'll be at his bank tomorrow morning! Let's go!

Wake up, Benny! We're there!

LORGELET BANK

Mr. Lorgelet? Ah! It's impossible at the moment! Mr. Lorgelet's in a meeting! If you'd wait a bit...

LOANS

Two hours later...

Mr. Lorgelet? Why, he's gone to lunch! He'll get back around three!

At three o'clock...

I'm sorry! Mr. Lorgelet's in a meeting! He cannot be disturbed for any reason!

For crying out loud! I'm getting fed up! Wait! I know a way to get in!

It's scandalous! I meant to open an account with several millions in this bank, and they keep me waiting! I've had it! I'm leaving!

LOANS

Don't-- don't leave, sir! I'll take you to Mr. Lorgelet's office!

9

This way! Mr. Lorgelet's awaiting you!

Dussiflard! What a surprise! I don't believe it...

Mister Lorgelet, I--

You're calling me "mister," now? Haha! Call me just Lorgelet, like in the good ol' days!

I've come about something very important and urgent--

Do you know I still play saxophone? You should hear me in "Body and Soul"--

Listen, Lorgelet, it's really, very important! Do you remember--

Mister Lorgelet, Mister Lorgelet, a gentleman's insisting on seeing you immediately... he's in the little office.

Excuse me, I'll just be a minute... Be right back, eh!

An hour later...

He doesn't come back very fast!

Indeed!

What are you doing here? The boss has left, you know! He always leaves at six on Fridays!

Why-- it's not possible! He knew we were here!

Ah?... Well, come! We'll ask the superintendent!

No, I didn't see him go by... And his car is still in the garage...

Something suspicious is going on! Benny, stay here... The superintendent and I will search everywhere!

12

Perhaps poor Lorgelet has had an attack! We absolutely must find him again! Let's go check upstairs!

He wouldn't be in the basement, by any chance?

We could always go take a look!

Follow me!

The safety deposit room is that way! You go, I'll check in the boiler-room.

Yoo-hoo! Monsieur Lorgelet!

Help me!

Is that you, Monsieur Lorgelet? Where are you?

I'm tied up in the vault! Some sticks of dynamite are going to blow up!

Wait! I'll go find the superintendent!

It won't do any good! Only my associate has the other set of keys! And the fuse has almost burnt up...! It's horrible! I-- I--

Okay! In that case, there's only one thing to do!

13

And that's the first trial of Benny Breakiron...

KROIING

KKKRRRAANG

Yikes! It's going to explode! And Mr. Lorgelet has fainted!...

Quick!

BOOOM

An explosion?!

It's downstairs!

Benny! Are you injured?

No, no! But we might need a pick-me-up for Monsieur Lorgelet!

What--what happened?...

A few drinks later...

...and threatening me with his revolver, that stranger forced me to lead him to the safety deposit room, where I'd been keeping the piece of the emir's paper!

He was certainly a man paid by Vercheval! We're all in danger! In fact, do you know what's become of the others?

No! I know that Piccolo--you remember him?-- has become a trainer in a circus! But I have no idea of where it's currently located!

Wait! I'll call an entertainment agency! Maybe they could tell me.

...That's right... Yes... Thank you, Miss!

We're in luck! The circus he works for is down south at the moment, in Barasson!

Okay! I'll leave this very evening!

12

14

Here's some money!... Yes, yes, I insist! Keep me apprised of your efforts!

Thanks, Lorgelet! Goodbye!

Goodbye! Good luck!

But-- but in fact, I was tied up in the vault... The door was armored... How was I able to get out of there?

A few hours later...

Monsieur Dussiflard! Careful!

Huh? What?... Oh! I think I dozed off!...

That's to be expected! You haven't slept in two days! You should get some rest!

You're right, Benny! Driving is dangerous when you're too tired! I'll take a nap for an hour or two...

We're losing time! Heaven knows if, at this very moment, that bandit Verchavel isn't stealing the paper from that Mr. Piccolo...

NNNz

I've got it!

NNNz

13

At dawn...
⇒Yawn!⇐ Let's go! We still have a ways before we arrive in Barasson!

Hey! Benny! Look! We-- we're here?!

BARASSON

I just don't understand! I'd have sworn I fell asleep halfway there!...

Really?

Hey! Why are those people running over there?

MARKET

PICCOLO CIRCUS

PICCOLO CIRCUS

BA

HELP!
A--A BEAR! IN CITY HALL!

?

EEEEEEEEEE!
I HAVE MONKEYS IN MY LIVING ROOM!

THERE'S A TIGER IN MY TANK!

What's going on?

AAH!

! !

BAR D

SCREEEEEE

16

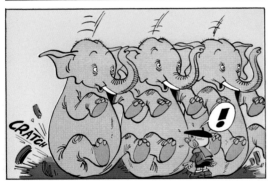

ROAAR

That mean beast tried to bite me!

GOK

Ah! There's the circus!

Voilà! And now you be good!

And you, too! Into your cage!

My goodness, all the animals are free! Who could have done that?

SLAM

And voilà! So long as it's shut in the trailer, that bear won't hurt anyone! I'll come back for him soon! Onto the others, now!

16

Ah! A lion!

GROAAR

BOOO!

All right, come on, lion! You must be good and get back into your cage!

Hey! Not into that trailer! There's already a bear!

Why-- there was somebody, too?! Hey, there! Leave that man alone, or else...

GRROW

As soon as I catch all the animals, I'll check on you, monsieur!

There's no sign of Piccolo! Too bad, we'll have to put down all the wild animals running free!

But the animals are all back in their cages! And that's the second trial of Benny Breakiron...

Benny?!...

Monsieur Dussiflard! Come quick! There's an unconscious man in the trailer over there!

19

A little later...

Piccolo! It's me, Dussiflard!

Dussiflard! Goodness!... I-- Oh! My head!

Are you better?

What happened, my old friend Piccolo?... We found you lying on the ground, and the animals from your zoo were running free!

Ah?... I-- Wait! This morning, I got a visit from a fellow coming on the behalf of Vercheval! You remember him, eh? He asked me if I still had my piece of the paper the emir had given us!

And did you give it to him?

No, no!... Next he asked me for a cup of coffee! I had one, too, and-- and then I don't remember anything else!

You were drugged!... Where's the paper?

There! In the drawer!

It's gone!

Ah! The bandit! And he tried to eliminate you by opening the animals' cages so they'd devour you!

But why did he want that paper anyhow? After all, it has no great value!

Yes, it does! Wait! I'll explain everything to you!

So, that's why! Ah! The bandit! Do you know where to find the others?

Alas, no! But Lorgelet told me he was going to look into it! Where can I make a call?

Hello, Lorgelet?... Yes, it's me! I found Piccolo, but too late! His paper was stolen from him! Yes!... And on your end? Ah!... Who's that?

Tronchu!... Yes, the clarinetist! He lives in Mougnies, up North! I'll give you his address!

Lorgelet has found Tronchu! Come quick, Benny, we have to get there before Vercheval attacks him!

18

All the localities of the mining region resemble one another, with their little, working class houses at the foot of slag heaps and the scaffolding of girders where the little wheels spin...

We're here, Benny!

I hope we didn't come too late this time!

Is Mr. Tronchu here, please?

Ah, no! He's at the colliery at this hour! If it's urgent, pop over there!

The engineer? One moment, I'll let him know! Who are you?

Dussiflard! Jules Dussiflard!

Mr. Tronchu's an engineer?

It seems so!

Tronchu!

Dussiflard! Old Dussiflard! How are you?

OFFICES →

Is this your son?

No! He's Benny! My good friend!

Bonjour, monsieur!

Ha! Ha! Ha! It makes me happy to see you again! What brings you here?

Oh! It's a long story! But first a question: do you still have your piece of the paper from the emir?

Ah! Yes! Of course! Why?

19.

Tronchu, you're in danger! Some criminals will do anything to get their paws on your paper!

Is this a joke? What do you think they'll do with it?

Mister Tronchu, there was an urgent call! You must go at once to the closed mine, at shaft 42!

Ah? Okay!

Come along! You can tell me all that on the way! And that'll let you visit the mine!

Cool!

So you understand, after Lorgelet, Piccolo, and me, they could attack you!

Let them come!

Still, I'd have never believed that of Vercheval!

Me either! And yet--

Rats! He's not going down alone! He has two people with him!

Too bad for them! It's too late now! The trap's been set!

Your paper's in a safe place, at least?

Well, no! It's at my home, in my office! I'll go put it in a safety deposit box at the bank right away!

Well? There's nobody here! What does that mean? Why did someone have me come here?

Hey, Monsieur Tronchu, did you see? There's a box here!

A box? What's it doing here?

BAROOM

GET DOWN! IT'S ALL COLLAPSING!

BOOOM

≑Whew!≑ It's over! Anyone hurt?

You okay, Benny?

Yes! But what happened?

We fell into an ambush! Look! The box was connected to a detonator!

The bandits!

We're lucky the whole gallery (1) didn't cave in! But, in the meantime, we're trapped!

Do-- do you think we'll get out?

Of course! The rescuers will arrive soon, you'll see!

Three hours later...

This waiting is annoying! Are you certain they're working on getting us out?

Yes, of course. Come on! Calm down!

24 hours later...

What the heck are they doing?

I'm thirsty, Monsieur Dussiflard!

Patience, Benny!

While on the surface...

There's no way to move forward! It keeps caving in! We'll continue, but there's not much hope...

And 36 hours later...

It's harder and harder to breathe! You think we still have a chance to get out?

Listen, don't tell the kid, but frankly, I'm afraid that if the rescuers don't reach us in a few hours, we're done for!

(1) A horizontal passage in an underground mine.

23

I have to find a way out of here!... Maybe-- Yes! I can try--

Ah! You're awake, my poor Benny? How do you feel?

Just fine, Monsieur Dussiflard!

Hey! Did you see? There's a little opening here!

I can just slip in!

No! Come back, Benny! It's too dangerous! It could cave in!

No, no! It'll be fine! Uh... I'm widening the opening a little!

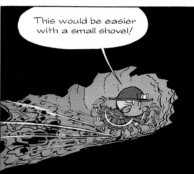

This would be easier with a small shovel!

Ouch! That's rock!

POW POW POW POW POW POW POW

Rats! I broke a fingernail!

Okay! To work!

They still haven't found the engineer?

No, alas! In my opinion they won't ever find them!

Hey! Oh! Heavens! What's happening? It's an earthquake!

Bonjour, ma'am, bonjour, m'sieur! Could you tell the rescuers to come help Mr. Dussiflard and Mr. Tronchu?

?!

?!

And that's the third trial of Benny Breakiron...

22

24

Later... Well, good ol' Dussiflard, we had a close call! It's lucky Benny found that tunnel out, otherwise ...

You think those ruffians took advantage of the time we were in the mine to snatch my paper?

I'm afraid so!

BERTHA!

Ah! Mister Tronchu! You're alive! Thank heavens! I thought you were dead!

Bertha! What happened?

Your paper, Tronchu?

I was coming back from the mine yesterday-- I was looking for news-- when some masked men attacked me! They put a rag under my nose, which smelled really bad... and then I don't remember anything else!

Oh! Mister Tronchu!

The paper's no longer here! They have three of them now, not counting that scoundrel Vercheval's!

Do you have news of the others?

Uh, no! I know that Van Overdekasslenbosch became an actor by the name of Boudingart, but I don't know where he is!

Wait! I'll call Lorgelet! Maybe he could give us some information!

He's going to look into it! He'll call me back!

And a few hours later...

DRIIIING DRIIIING

Ah! That must be him!

Hello?... Yes!... Ah! You found him?... Yes, I'm jotting it down! What's that?... Djondus? Where's that?... What?... IN SCANDINAVIA?!

We're lucky Mr. Lorgelet put this plane at our disposal, eh, Monsieur Dussiflard?

Bah!... I prefer my taxi!

Fasten your seatbelts, we're landing!

At last!

Do you feel better, Monsieur Dussiflard?

Uh... Yes, yes! Let's find a taxi!

To the Municipal Theater! Quick!

Ah! It must be here!

Come, Benny! Let's try to find the stage entrance!

NOW PLAYING
EDMOND ROSTAND'S
CYRANO DE BERGERAC
STARRING
BOUDINGART

Them again! We'll have to take action this very night!

It's there! Let's go in!

STAGE DOOR

HEY, THERE! WHERE'RE YOU GOING?

I must see Mr. Boudingart! It's urgent!

No way! The show's getting started! Wait outside!

But it's very important! It's a matter of life and death!

Not happening! I have my orders! Go on! Get out!

24

Stage manager! Where's the stage manager?

Curtain in three minutes!

Pardon me, ma'am, I'm looking for Monsieur Boudingart!

He's still up there, young man! Dressing room #3.

Ah! It's here!

Enter!

NOK NOK NOK

Monsieur, I--

Kid, I'm very, very busy! I'm going on stage in a few minutes! If you want an autograph, wait till the end of the show!

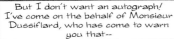

But I don't want an autograph! I've come on the behalf of Monsieur Dussiflard, who has come to warn you that--

Dussiflard? He's here?

Boudingart! Quick, my friend! We're waiting for you!

Listen, give this note to the box office! They'll let you into the theater! And tell Dussiflard to join me after the show, in the lobby of my hotel, across from the stage door!

Yes, M'sieur Boudingart!

On stage for the opening!

Monsieur Dussiflard! Monsieur Boudingart gave me a note for us to see the play! He'll wait for us after the show!

?!

Everyone ready? Okay! Let's go!

After the show...

That was good, eh, Monsieur Dussiflard? Do you think he was really dead at the end?

Why, no, Benny! It's acting!

Hey! Boudingart! Are you coming to the city's reception?

Sorry, mon cher, I must meet an old friend!

Why-- who are you? What are you doing in my dressing room?

Later...

Van Overdekassulebosch is really taking his time getting here! I'm starting to worry!

Monsieur Dussiflard! Look!

It looks like-- Heavens! The theater's on fire!

Let's hope Boudingart has gotten out!

There's the concierge! Let's ask him!

No, I don't remember seeing him leaving! And it's no longer possible to check! The fire has spread over the whole stage!

WOOOOO WOOOOO

Good work! Here's the sum agreed upon!

Poor fellow! If he's still in there, he's doomed!

26

28

Benny!
Where's Benny?

I'm certain Mr. Boudingart is still inside! I absolutely must save him!

Yikes!
There's no way to go forward!

There's only one thing to do--

¿Huff!¿

Benny exhales a powerful blast...

PFFFFFFOOU

...and blows out the fire like you blow out a candle or an oil well that's on fire.

What? It looks like the fire's decreasing in intensity!

Ah! There are the firemen!

Benny!
Benny!

WoooOooo
WoooOooo

And voilà! Quick!
To Monsieur Boudingart's dressing room!

I was right!
He was here!

HEY LOOK! There's a kid coming out of the theater! He saved someone!

Benny, where were you?

I went to look for your friend, Monsieur Dussiflard!

Well, yes! The fire's out! I don't understand it either!

29

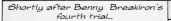

Shortly after Benny Breakiron's fourth trial...

Hello, Boss?... I have Boudingart's piece of paper!... No, he was saved at the last minute!... He's in his room with Dussiflard and the kid... Okay, I'll deal with it.

Well, I never! You're right! Before setting the theater on fire, they stole my little lucky-charm paper!

You understand why I'm trying to find all our buddies from the band! Vercheval's paying bandits to reassemble the entire deed!

I've already found Lorgelet, Piccolo, Tronchu and you! But I don't know where the others are!

Now that I think about it, when I came back from my triumphant tour in North Africa, I saw Delbouille! He was a cook on the ship!

Joseph?!...

Do you remember, Benny? Joesph! The cook on the freighter on which we were forcibly carried away by Hairynose? (1)

Oh, yes! The bearded guy! That's him?

And what boat is he working on now?

On the "Ville de Fert," which sails between Marseille and Port Ahmed!

Okay! We'll leave tomorrow morning for Marseille! I'll call the airport to find out if our plane is still there!

All right! I know enough!

Hello? Connect me to the airport, please!...

Understand? It's the little plane at the end of the runway!

And the next day...

(1) See BENNY BREAKIRON #1 "The Red Taxis."

Yes, I called this shipping company this morning! The boat Joseph's on will dock in Part Ahmed tomorrow evening!

We could-- **HEY!** What's going on?

The controls aren't responding! I'm no longer in control of the plane!

WHAT?!

Quick! Grab the parachutes in the rear compartment!

But there's nothing here!

That's not possible! They were still there yesterday evening... Heavens! We're doomed!

This is Vercheval's doing!

He's gotten us! What'll we do?

I'll try to land, but we have only one chance out of a thousand of getting out of this alive!

This is no time to catch a cold!

But that's horrible! I don't want to die!

Shut up! Let me pilot!

There's only one way to save all three of us!

GO!

N017K

THOOM

Yikes! It's going to crash!

Quick, quick, quick!...

?!

Oh! Sorry!

Excuse me, I have to catch up with a plane!

AAAAH! PULL UP! PULL UP!

There's no way! It's the end!

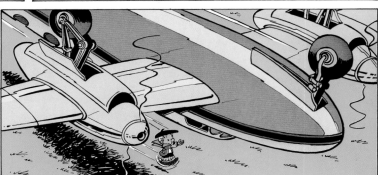

Got it!

Why-- why we're not dead?!

Benny? Where's Benny?

And that's the fifth trial of Benny Breakiron.

A bit later...

That's it, all right! Someone snipped the command wiring!

Yes, there's a train station three miles from here! But the last train's coming through in an hour!

Hang on, Monsieur Dussifland! We're almost there!

≥Pffff!≤... ≥Pffff!≤...

What the--?! Did you forget to release the brakes? We're not moving!

Hurry! I'll hold the train back!

What a cattle car! Luckily we're changing at the next station!

Hurry! We're going to miss the connection!

We'll go directly to the airport upon arriving!

What? There's no plane for Port Ahmed for two days?

And two days later...

Ah! We're arriving! You see the port down there? The "Ville de Fert" must be one of those ships!

Hey! Joseph!

There's a fellow on deck who wants to talk to you! He says he's here on the behalf of a certain "Vercheval."

·31·

33

Quick! To the port!

Let's hope Vercheval hasn't already had time to act!

VILLE DE FERT

Pardon me, sir, I'm looking for Joseph the cook!

Again!...

A half-hour ago, some guy came looking for him! I heard them talking about a piece of paper! Joseph went to look for it in his cabin and left with the guy.

They got into a speedboat! Hey, that's it heading off over yonder!

Heavens! Let's go alert the port police! They have to catch them!

Well, no! They might arrive too late!

I'll take care of it myself!

Poor Joseph! He's fallen into a trap! Quick, Benny!

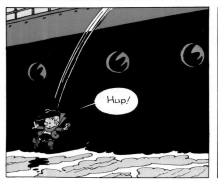

Hup!

Where on earth are you taking me?

Don't worry--

32

That boat goes fast! But I'll catch up!

We're far enough from the coast! Go ahead!

But--

Good! Now, stuff him in a sack and throw him overboard!

Hey! What's happening?

Why are we going backwards?!

Curd! What are you doing? Are you crazy? Put it in forward gear!

But I'm in forward gear! And the motors are on full! I-- I don't understand!/...

It's simple, however, what can 1100hp do against Benny's strength? And that's his sixth trial.

Okay! We're reaching the port!

35

So, after taking my paper, they forced me onto their boat! I think they intended to throw me overboard!

Bandits! Give us back that paper!

We no longer have it! We gave it to a fellow dressed all in black who'd paid us to do this job!

Ah! Monsieur Joseph, you're safe!

Benny! Why you're soaked! Did you fall in the water?

Come quick and dry off in my cabin!

You understand, Joseph, that bandit Vercheval is trying to get for himself all the fragments of the deed for our land ever since he found out oil was found there!

There remains only Lahuchette and Saint-Amand du Riflaud who still have their papers... if they've haven't already been victimized by that scoundrel Vercheval!

Do you know where they are?

No! But we'll call Lorgelet, the banker. He's asked all of his branches to search for the members of our band!

Yes, transfer him to me!... Dussiflard? So, did you find Joseph?... Arrived too late? Good heavens!... Listen, I have Lahuchette's address! No! I distrust the phone!... That's right! Catch the first plane!... See you tomorrow!

Lorgelet's found Lahuchette's address! But he didn't want to tell it to me over the phone! He's afraid of indiscretions!

Come! Let's go reserve two seats on the next plane!

Hello, Boss? Dussiflard and the kid are returning to Lorgelet's! He knows where Lahuchette is, but he said nothing, because he's starting to get mistrustful!... Yes! Okay!

Hours later....

Hi!

We came about the phone!

Oh?

5%

...and cancel all my appointments for tomorrow! I'm expecting someone!

Yes, Mister Lorgelet!

DRIIING DRIIING

Yes?... What?... But my telephone works just fine!... Okay, send them up!

Will it be long?

No, no sir! We'll only be a minute!

We're just checking!

There! It's in good order! Goodbye, sir!

⸴Hmm!⸴ Goodbye!

And the next day...

Dussiflard! Benny! I'm happy to see you again!

How are you, Lorgelet?

Good! I didn't tell you anything on the phone because I'm starting to worry about spies! Here, at least, nobody can hear us!

I found Lahuchette's trail! He's leading an archeological expedition at Khben-Nogbang, in the Far East!

38

Khben-Nogbang, a little town in Southeast Asia, that blends the picturesque charm of the Far East with the benefits of Western civilization...

Ah! There's the European Club! I was told we'd find the consul there!

You're looking for the Lahuchette Expedition? By the devil, it won't be easy to reach it! It's 250 miles from here in the middle of the jungle!

There's a train tomorrow morning that goes to Dhurth-Noglang! There, you can find a guide for the rest of the trip!

They're going to take the train for Dhurth-Noglang!

Good! Arrange it so that they won't arrive alive!

Since you have time, maybe we could have a golf match?

With pleasure!

Could I try, too, M'sieur?

Of course!

Hold your club firmly like this... there! And you hit it very hard!

Hello, NASA, I've discovered a curious round, white meteorite! You won't believe me if I tell you what it looks like!

The next day...

Say, Monsieur Dussiflard...

Yes, Benny?...

How is it that we're all alone in this car, when the others are packed?

Because we're in first class, and the locals are too poor to pay for this luxury for themselves!

Let's go! You take care of unhooking the cars!

Understood!

Slow this train down! Come on, quick! Or else--

And there!

All done!

Okay! Now put the steam at full power and then *JUMP!* Quick!

TCHUFF TCHUFF TCHUFF TCHUFF

38

40

Ah! Monsieur Dussiflard has fallen asleep!

RRZ ZZZ

I'll take this opportunity to go on a little tour!

!

But-- the other cars have been detached!

Sapristi! It's like in "The Adventures of Tintin!" I bet the bandits mean to cause an accident!

I'm right! The engineers have abandoned the engine!

I've got to stop this train before it derails! But where's the brake? Maybe it's this lever here?

WOOOEEEEEE

TCHUFF TCHUFF

PSHEEEEEEEE

It won't work! Not like this at least!

So...

TCHUFF TCHUFF TCHUFF

39

Heavens! That was a close call! Where are the engineers?

They must have jumped off while it was running! It's another of Vercheval's tricks!

You think?... Meanwhile, I wonder how we'll...

VRRRR ?

We're saved! It's a military convoy!

What happened?

We just escaped an assassination attempt! We'd taken the train to rejoin my friend Lahuchette who--

What? Lahuchette? Hands up?

But--

They're two accomplices of the spy we're looking for, Colonel! They blew up the train!

Load 'em up!

But that's false! We--

I assure you we're not spies! It's a man named Vercheval who--

SILENCE!

Ah! Here's Dhurth-Noglang! Stop in front of the military outpost!

Yes, two terrorists! Interrogate them closely! I want to have signed confessions upon my return!

Yes, Colonel!

Come now, I've told you--

Move out! We must arrive at Lahuchette's camp before nightfall!

I'll question the kid first! Take away the man with the mustache!

Don't worry, Benny! It'll be all right!

Okay! Just us, kid! You're going to tell me everything you know about Lahuchette! Got it?

Yes, m'sieur!

Here goes! Some bandits want to steal from him his piece of paper from he emir and--

The emir? What emir?

The one who'd come to listen to the band! And they released tigers and elephants because Vercheval, who was one of Monsieur Dussiflard's friends, but who isn't any longer, wants to keep...

...the oil all for himself! And they also sabotaged the airplane after the theater fire, but I saved everyone because I'm very strong. And when the boat--

Three hours later...

If I understand you right, someone stole a boat at the bottom of a coal mine located in a bank vault, where there was a billionaire animal tamer performing Cyrano de Bergerac...!

But, no! Cyrano de Bergerac is the fire!

ENOUGH!

I can't take it anymore! Take him away!

And M'sieur Lahuchette? Will they bring him here?

Aspirin

No! He's a spy! The patrol that went to look for him will execute him immediately!

GLAG

!

It's not possible! He's certainly innocent! It's another of Vercheval's tricks!

GLAG

I have to go save him!

SCRANTCH

42.

44

Luckily the tracks from the tank treads is still visible! I'll just have to follow it!

Meanwhile, a few miles away...

Night's falling, Singh... Light the lamp and prepare the meal!

Ah! I'll-- Hello! Sounds like a motor noise...

RRRRR

My goodness! Military trucks! What are they coming to do here?

Welcome, gentlemen. My name is Lahuchette, and I--

And you're caught, Mister Lahuchette! Hands up!

Me? A spy? Come now, that's ridiculous! I--

Search his tent!

Yes, Colonel!

I hope I'll find that much talked-about piece of paper. He told me he'd give me a thousand dollars!... Ah! There's his wallet!

And here's the paper!... Now I just have to replace it with the microfilms!

And this, eh? And this? Microfilms stolen from the War Ministry, is this not proof? Enough! You'll be shot tomorrow at dawn!

Sapristi! Night falls quickly here! I almost don't see traces of the tracks anymore!

43

46

Rats! Too late!

Unless...

Aim...

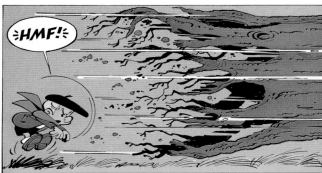

≿HMF!≾

I'm innocent!... No! Don't fire! No!

FIRE!

BANG BANG
BANG BANG
BANG BANG

And that's Benny Breakiron's 8th trial.

?

They-- they missed me?!

? ? ? ? ? ?

Stop! M'sieur Lahuchette is innocent! I'm sure of it!

?

That kid again! Where'd he come from? Seize him!

Ah! Careful! I'm strong! Very strong!

45

47

All right! All of you out of there!

Oww!

Nobody left?

Okay! Now I just have to take care of that machine gun!

And I hate machine guns!

SCRUNCH

And that's Benny Breakiron's 9th trial.

Now I'll be able to rescue that poor M'sieur Lahuchette!

I swear to you you're making a mistake!...

VRRRRR?

All right then! A helicopter now!

Mercy!

That kid is the devil! I'd better run away! After all, I have the much-talked about piece of paper! That's the main thing!

47

A few days later...

After our arrival, we'll go to Lorgelet's bank! Maybe he has news!

Happy to see you again, my friends! In fact, I'm awaiting a call from one of my informants.

DRING

Ah! There!

What? Ah! You know where Saint-Amand du Riflaud is.

What? The viscount? He's -- He's become -- My goodness!

Incredible! Viscount Saint-Amand du Riflaud is in Beuville... he's become a hobo!...

We'll depart immediately in pursuit!

We'll depart immediately in pursuit!

Once we're in town, Dussiflard, we'll split up...

A hobo named Saint-Amand du Riflaud? Are you joking or what?

What if you asked at lost-and-found?

No, no detainee answers to the name of Saint-Amand...

Sounds like a wine to us!

Ha! Ha!

Surely that must remind you of something?... A hobo who's a viscount, no?

You really want to know what that reminds us of?

Be polite with the gentleman! He's friend with the nobility!

Ar--- ⇒hic!⇐ -stocrats, off with their heads!

SOUP KITCHEN

Well?

And Benny?

Nothing! Not the slightest trace!

You're very kind, kid... ⇒sniff!⇐ ...to have gotten old man La Cloppe a little firewood to burn! ⇒Sniff!⇐ I wasn't warm, and I've got one of those colds!

So, you're looking for the viscount? ⇒Sniff!⇐ ... Okay! Well, come with me! We'll find him for you!

Hey, Rillette! You haven't ⇒sniff!⇐ ... seen the viscount today?

Viscount? Ain't he over on the West Side?

We'd find the Unknown Soldier's name for you for that sum! Come on, Joe, we're going hobo hunting!

RIVER

The viscount? Did you go look over by the warehouses?

Well? You tell us where he is, or do we put you through the grinder?

Eight o'clock! And Benny still isn't at the rendezvous!

Don't you worry, ⸮sniff!⸮ -- we'll end up finding him!

The vis- ⸮hic!⸮ viscount? ⸮Hic!⸮ Saw him go by not five minutes ago! W-- ⸮hic!⸮ Two fellows taking him into the buil-- ⸮hic!⸮ Buildings under construction!

Gentlemen, I'd like to know where you're taking me!

Go on, Joe! Search the viscount!

Come now, gentlemen...

There's the piece of paper!

Good!

Give me that back!

We're done with him! Get rid of him, Joe!

Gentlemen, I protest!

POW

Come quick! Let's escape before those who pushed me realize I'm still alive!

÷Sniff!÷ That's it! Old man La Cloppe has given me his cold! Luckily it didn't happen a few seconds earlier, or else--

Come this way! Monsieur Dussiflard's waiting for us!

Dussiflard? Dear old Dussiflard?... How--?

Dussiflard! Lorgelet! Lahuchette! Wow! I can't believe it's you!

And what an astonishing coincidence! You'll never guess what just happened to me!

Yes! Someone tried to knock you off after stealing from you your paper from the emir!

How did you know?

We'll explain to you later! We'll first get a few hours of rest at my home!

Say, Monsieur Dussiflard, I've caught a cold, It's awful, isn't it?

No, Benny, a cold isn't anything very serious!

But when I have a cold, I lose all my strength and--

I say, Saint-Amand...

It's no use insisting, he'll never believe me...

The next morning...

...and that bandit Vercheval now possesses all our papers!

Ah, no! Not mine!

What'll we do?

ATCHOOO!

I have a plan, but for that, I'd need all the others to be here! Lorgelet, can you contact Boudingart, Piccolo, and Joseph to come as quickly as possible?

A few days later...

My dear old Van Overdekassulenbosch!

Boudingart! They call me Boudingart nowadays!

Come now, Saint-Amand! Leave those butts alone!

Piccolo? Good, show him in!

PICCOLO!

My friends, I'm so happy see you!

Okay, now that we're all here, I'll explain my plan to you! To get the oilfield, the bandits now need only one piece of the emir's deed! The one that I possess...

I propose that we all go to Vivejoie-la-Grande and that I serve as bait! With all of us together, we'll capture them and get back what belongs to us!

Monsieur Dussiflard, don't do anything before my cold is over, or else I won't be able to protect you!

Why yes, Benny! Get ready, we're leaving!

Like all the provincial towns, Vivejoie-la-Grande peacefully falls asleep at nightfall...

No, Benny, don't insist: it's late, and you should go home and get some good sleep!

But, Monsieur Dussiflard...

All right, don't worry about me, my plan is foolproof! Get going!

Yes, Monsieur Dussiflard.

I'm worried. I really want to--

Oh! Well, why not, then? Disobeying isn't good, but I'm going to follow him anyway!

56

Scoundrel! We've finally got you! **HERE, MY FRIENDS!**

Dussiflard! But--

Lorgelet!... Piccolo!... But how--?

You're going to give back what you stole from us!

Wretched traitor! Your time has come!

Listen to me! I don't know what's happened since I was abducted by the "Big Petroleum Company"! It was the day that I met you, Dussiflard! They took my paper from me and locked me in a basement!

If they let me go to join you this evening, it can only be a trap!

Exactly! Hands up and drop your weapons!

Move out quick!

It's awful! They're taking them away! And I can't do anything!

Luckily I heard everything! So it's the "Big Petroleum Company," the bandits!

Quick, I must alert the police!

...and at this hour, you should already be in bed!

That's no use! It's always the same, those policemen never believe little boys!

56.

58

Dawn rises over the imposing building of the "Big Petroleum Company..."

And there! Now we possess the nine fragments of the deed! Where are the former owners of the oilfield?

In a safe place! We'll get rid of them a little later!

It's here!

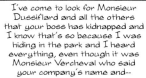

Merci beaucoup for bringing me, Monsieur!

Goodbye, kid!

Hey! Just where do you think you're going?

I've come to look for Monsieur Dussif'lard and all the others that your boss has kidnapped and I know that's so because I was hiding in the park and I heard everything, even though it was Monsieur Vercheval who said your company's name and--

Go on! Get! Scram, you little brat!

I won't be able to do anything so long as I have this rotten head cold!

WAK

ZOOOOM

?

KREEEN KRESH

EUM COMPANY

Yippee! My cold's cured, now we'll see about that!

Sorry!

And now I'll put this precious paper in a safe place and--

What's that noise? There's nobody in the building... Today's Sunday!

Monsieur Duss-- ah! I recognize you! You're the one who abducted Monsieur Dussiflard! Where is he?

Who's the kid?

It's Dussiflard's buddy! I got this!

Oh, really?

POW

Why that's the emir's paper! Give me that!

And now, tell me where you've hidden Monsieur Dussiflard and his friends, you bandits!

But we don't know what you mean, kid... You must be mistaken...

If you don't tell me, I warn you, I'll break everything!

Sure you will kid!

Ah! You don't believe me! Well come on, you'll see!

So you swear to me nobody's in your building!

No, nobody... Why?...

56

And you still refuse to tell me where you took Monsieur Dussiflard and his friends?... All right, you asked for it!

What will you do?

WAK

WAK CRRRRR

And that's Benny Breakiron's eleventh trial...

BRROOOM

My building!

! !

Now tell me where Monsieur Dussiflard is or I'll--

No! I'll tell everything! I'll drive you! Don't hit me!

This time, we're well and truly doomed. The "Big Petroleum Company" is holding all the cards!

Shh! Someone's coming!

CRONC

Benny! They have you, too--?

Everything's all right, Monsieur Dussiflard! It's all taken care of, you're free!

And look! I even have the emir's paper!

59

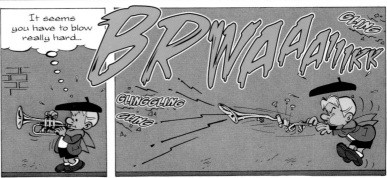

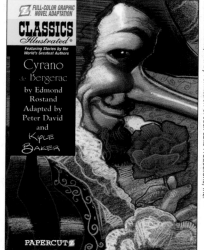

Welcome to the thrilling, trial-filled, timeless, third BENNY BREAKIRON graphic novel, written by Yvan Delporte and Peyo and illustrated by Peyo and François Walthéry, from Papercutz. We're the Benny-sized comics company dedicated to publishing great graphic novels for all ages. Graphic novels such as those created by Pierre Culliford, better known as Peyo: THE SMURFS, THE SMURFS ANTHOLOGY (which also features *Johan and Peewit*), THE SMURFS CHRISTMAS, and of course, BENNY BREAKIRON.

I'm Jim Salicrup, the Editor-in-Chief and Peyo aficionado who can never get enough Peyo comics! That's probably because I also happen to really love all the other wonderful comics Papercutz publishes, and there's just so many hours in the day!

But it's interesting when the various Papercutz titles happen to overlap a little bit. For example, in this very BENNY BREAKIRON graphic novel, Benny and Monsieur Dussiflard had to race Scandinavia to catch the actor Boudingart, formerly known as Van Overdekasslenbosch, before the bad guys get to him. Boudingart is starring in a production of Cyrano de Bergerac, a play that's filled with just as much humor and adventure as a BENNY BREAKIRON graphic novel.

In fact, Papercutz published an excellent adaptation of Edmond Rostand's famous work in CLASSICS ILLUSTRATED #10 "Cyrano de Bergerac." It was adapted by the award-winning team of Peter David, writer, and Kyle Baker, artist—two of the most talented guys in comics today. If you don't have this incredible graphic novel, I'm happy to report that it's still available on Papercutz.com! CLASSICS ILLUSTRATED is the legendary comics series that features stories by the world's greatest authors, and adapted into comics by great comics writers and artists. If you like BENNY BREAKIRON, I know you'll love "Cyrano de Bergerac"! Best of all, there's zero chance of the theater burning down, if you get a graphic novel instead!

And don't forget, Benny Breakiron will be back in BENNY BREAKIRON #4 "Uncle Placid"!

Merci,

Jim

STAY IN TOUCH!
EMAIL: Salicrup@papercutz.com
WEB: www.papercutz.com
TWITTER: @papercutzgn
FACEBOOK: PAPERCUTZGRAPHICNOVELS
SNAIL MAIL: Papercutz, 160 Broadway,
    Suite 700, East Wing, New York, NY 10038

"The characters that I've created are not tough guys at the outset. They become strong together, by being united."

— *PEYO*

Over 50 years ago, a Belgian cartoonist known as Peyo set his pencil to a blank page and created a worldwide phenomenon we know as The Smurfs. Join us in celebrating more than a half century of humor, camaraderie, heroism, and heart. Experience the master at his best.

THE WONDER OF PEYO

INCOMPARABLE NEW GRAPHIC NOVELS FROM **PAPERCUT**Z™

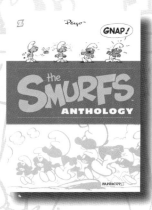